CW00732856

Gallery Books
Editor: Peter Fallon

COLLECTED POEMS

Pearse Hutchinson

COLLECTED POEMS

Gallery Books

Collected Poems
is first published simultaneously
in paperback and hardback
on 16 February 2002.

The Gallery Press
Loughcrew
Oldcastle
County Meath
Ireland

ISBN 1 85235 312 0 (*paperback*)
1 85235 313 9 (*clothbound*)
1 85235 314 7 (*limited signed edition*)

A CIP catalogue record for this book
is available from the British Library.

The Gallery Press acknowledges the financial assistance
of An Chomhairle Ealaíon / The Arts Council, Ireland,
and the Arts Council of Northern Ireland.

Contents

COLLECTED POEMS

Changes

for Huyck van Leeuwen and Judith Herzberg

A crouched ancient in a hooker-doon sparring
with a laughing schoolboy, satchel spurned into shadow,
gleaming barber and grimed garage-hand
watching; the crazy corner-swaying of tall
green buses; green lead soldiers on a lawn
deployed in exultant play by three small
quadroons: Today they seem entirely innocent,
these that could be images of death and risk
look now images of life and luck.

Look now peace, in the calmness of the sun
that makes most any barren or barbarous country
worth all your money and a lifelong journey;
look as tranquil and offer as much courage
as a black child playing with white in a Paris gutter,
as a young whore half in love one drunken summer,
looked and gave; tomorrow, if there's rain,
or under sunlight if my humour change,
or the humour changes of the men who rule us,

They may recover their more usual look,
of apparently bearable pain one form of brute
gives another; why even my high hope humour
in Paris came to grief, with, scratched on a urinal,
'Mort aux noirs, comme aux juifs!' To pluck up goodness
of dandelion or honesty to lapels is duty
ill appeased. How seldom deft is any man
whose quick brain tries to marry the haggard heart —
why even a thing like rain can change his reading

of pleasant children into green lead bleeding.

Petition to Release

for Bert Achong

And they all go winding assiduously watches —
tiny, jewelled informers, time-jailers
(for time walked round, whipped round a prison-yard,
must find it hard, never achieving oblivion,
telling the world: Wait! and patting pillows).

And they all go winding deciduously watches —
for every twist of the wrist is a leaf loosened,
a life lessened, a lesson learnt, a letter burnt;
the tick-talk may gloss across the losing,
but not the loss. Who can fasten back the leaf?
relive the life? or forget the lesson?
or look at the letter unsigned as it puzzled the anguish
of the angry or penitent lover, while his watch
muttered warnings of late mornings, the witch?

I don't know who the hell could get me to work,
a black boy goes boasting beside Mayaro Bay.
They may all go winding aciduously watches,
but I don't know who the hell could get me to work,
for I'm sweet, not bitter — nor the sea to work,
for it's strong, not petty. But the princess-pretty
thoughts you wear, singer, in your soft blue hair
we share behind our chained wrists and
our winding, assiduous, bitter, brittle days.
For someone stupid like a station-master,
a competent rebel, or a duck-faced emperor,
invented once in a wicked whoopee
espionage and prison against our friend —
el tiempo: amigo mio, nuestro amado.
And all the little ingredients went winding
themselves assiduously up, and finding fun.

Tempus Tyrannus, Tempus Rex,
only wears a crown upon his soft blue hair
(to hide it, so that wise-men declare him decrepit)
when the glass dungeons close out the sun
and the river and the white white girl with a rose
in her soft gold hair and the grinning beggar;
and they all go (the jewelled and brainless jailers),
winding
            assiduously
                        watches
                                    deciduously
                                                chuckling.

A Folly

A self-styled misanthrope, who wrote perfect pentameters,
but was not in many ways truly conformist,
wanted to build the kind of tower that used to be of ivory
in the days when ivory was cheap.
He couldn't afford it, so he used
black brick instead.
Nevertheless, he passed an Act of Will whereby the tower
would be described as ivory;
he was not so much in pursuit of truth as in flight from
those in flight from it.
When the tower was built, it looked magnificent —
Castilho would have envied it, so would Oscar Niemeyer —
and he hadn't forgotten the central heating, or the stairs.
There was a built-in genie who could do everything,
including the Varisara, quetzal-minting,
and the abolition of Esperanto.

But for some reason —
magic as the amenities were —
it proved uninhabitable.
So before he got into the hunt again
he tried to palm it off on someone,
as a present or at a price.
A friend said: 'What, that poky little Nissen hut —
why you couldn't swing a seraglio in it!'
An acquaintance cried: 'Surely in the 20th century
we've got beyond believing in the supernatural!'
Nor would anyone buy it.
A legend quickly developed among the local people —
there always are local people, even in the biggest desert —
that the tower was haunted.
Shuilers gave it a wide berth.
So he left it to rack and ruin, lacking even the heart
to write in the snow outside
his name, with an apostrope s and the word *Folly*;
and re-entered the hunt (or flight).

A Man

A man is screaming in his bathroom,
and the neighbours mistake it for singing.
The door is locked, the windows barred,
but the noise goes through the walls,
and the neighbours mistake it for singing.
One says: 'He hasn't a note in his head,'
another: 'He sounds happy, the monster,'
and a foreigner strolling in the street below
marvels: 'What exuberance, what brio
these people have!'
                 What noise
can the man himself think he is making?

Bulletin

The mean amount of courage man's allowed
by merely breathing, by his own prim will,
becomes quite soon more undependable still
if he imagined, being young and proud,
that freedom should not only be avowed
in private chat and public verse but tracked
by the warm hand each day: such whims attract
the mindless fury of the stampeding crowd.

Or money and lovers (pretended liberties) will
demand he at least negotiate for a pact
with safety-third and horse-magog sense, and kill
the young spontaneous innocent daring: till
compromises between excessive tact
and skulking defiance make his meanest fact.

The Nuns at the Medical Lecture

The nuns at the medical lecture have rose faces
like babies surprised into wisdom, the clerical students
passing the pub look slightly scared, but mainly
serene, the cultured ancient cod in his lamplit room
lined with the desert fathers and the village idiots
and the palace pornographs, warms the port in his palm
and remarks that passion rages most after innocence
because it is innocent, and rages to corrupt;
the young spongers gape, consoling themselves
for the gap between drinks by considering sagacity,
we all sometimes talk like a tenth-rate
so understanding confessor.

Always the maligned force that carries light
achieves its kind revenge, and the velveteen shield
of every proud prig erupts in termed lunacy;
the man in dark glasses was, fancy, at the very same
college a vague few years ago, and buys the boy
a pint; the foreign landlady sends in coffee
at odd hours and doesn't charge it;
the brilliant friend suddenly weeps, and pity
does the trick; the adolescent skeleton
mariconettes in front of the glistening wardrobe;
the nun fingertips her scraped pate with pride,
and the masseur, the barber, the preacher, and the prior . . .

So like whiskey creates anger, and love creates greed,
as the lizard creates the sun, and the bull sand,
we have created your sin, we conceived
the death of your innocence.
With all our ageing need, we have corrupted you,
as the air corrupts the bud into flower,
as the fountain corrupts the air.
Let us go, and you in front with sackcloth and ashes
over silk, and lament the beautiful ivory death

all would have walked through had we not met —
in a carnival of personal pronouns, a battle of flowers
and roots, wear this laughter to shreds.

Eight Frontiers Distant

for John Jordan

Eight frontiers distant
from the company and gesture of his true friends,
each man becomes less perfect in affection.
Divided by a hundred seas and lakes
from the second-rate, the tenth-rate, and the unspeakable,
each man recalls their faces and their names
with gradually less disdain.
Travel is in this matter, so,
more specious than trite death.
Till, having crossed back over two frontiers,
or ten extensive deserts of water,
confronted suddenly at a café-table
with choice between his own alone integrity,
with all its dangerous peepshows,
and the fourth- or fifteenth-rate with an eager face,
and a Nansen passport somewhere in the background,
each man hears need, putting on the voice of duty,
re-assert itself; and into his mind again
his true friends come,
smiling and loving and mercilessly absent.

The River

The white swans and the single celestial black
manoeuvred with dignity out of our way as we glided
over the pond in the park.
And the less dexterous humans, with whom we collided,
laughed and shouted and smiled.

I sat at the rudder in my Sunday rig-out;
my uncle rowed and grunted at the long, splashing oars,
that shot up jets of water, jets of jewelled water,
to fasten as beads on his ginger mustachios,
and he longed for the voyage to be over.

Two aunts perched upright, idle, talkative, witty;
they fingered their spinster-finery now and again . . .
I relished an ice-cream cone, and thought of the river:
the great, broad river of ships, that seared like a topaz
    flame
the land of mountain and plain.

Field-Work

Effectual dandysmo, rags full of silica,
sex-appeal, grotesquerie, wit, wisdom, the secret of
'unendurable ecstasy interminably prolonged',
a true vision of art's climax the moment before speech,
knowledge, resentment, serenity, or even intelligence:
having not one of these, he only, of all that we met
among those many men, prostrated, in tiny clearings,
before unfinished images of Paresse,
gripped the defiant perfection of utter uselessness;
and that we envied more than anything in any world.
Yet we had to forget his existence before we could love him.

Travel Notes

Some men are scarcely conscious of
more than their own parishes yet
could hurt no foreigner nor scorn the strangest;
but they are few not many, let
no prideful island take
them for a sanction of each new mistake.

Some, through visiting many countries,
have grown less cocky on self, birth-place,
and glittering tags, while more sure of the earth;
but they're not many, you couldn't base
much hope, on them, for those
who know what time all bars in Europe close.

Two foreigners in a century,
perhaps, break through to a nation's core:
to them, honour; let grateful others take
some personal boons, and claim no more;
respect and love dispense
at once with blindness and omniscience.

Two foreigners — and how many
nationals, balladeers?

Málaga

for Sammy Sheridan

The scent of unseen jasmine on the warm night beach.

The tram along the sea road all the way from town
through its wide open sides drank unseen jasmine down.
Living was nothing all those nights but that strong flower,
whose hidden voice on darkness grew to such mad power
I could have sworn for once I travelled through full peace
and even love at last had perfect calm release
only by breathing in the unseen jasmine scent,
that ruled us and the summer every hour we went.

The tranquil unrushed wine drunk on the daytime beach.
Or from an open room all that our sight could reach
was heat, sea, light, unending images of peace;
and then at last the night brought jasmine's great release —
not images but calm uncovetous content,
the wide-eyed heart alert at rest in June's own scent.

In daytime's humdrum town from small child after child
we bought cluster on cluster of the star flower's wild
white widowed heads, re-wired on strong weed stalks
    they'd trimmed
to long green elegance; but still the whole month brimmed
at night along the beach with a strong voice like peace;
and each morning the mind stayed crisp in such release.

Some hint of certainty, still worth longing I could teach,
lies lost in a strength of jasmine down a summer beach.

Tomar

The lamb ran out, called, posed beneath a white rose-bush.
The famous rose-window was no Notre Dame.
The stone-dead Christ in his glass box blurred by flowered
    gauze.
The busy beata couldn't say which altar the bishop was
    buried
in front of, the notable tiles had been taken away
to be done something to. The rose-bush hung impassive,
whiter than the white self-advertising lamb.
The dogs went by muzzled in the heat of the fair-day,
the peasants clumped purposeful in fur collars, clutching
rolled black umbrellas like weapons and fetishes; loquats
ridiculous fruit and olives black and shiny as the hair
of the smart young men jostled in the marketplace,
a busker was very amusing for hours at the expense of
a sheepish grinning boy who bore it for one-and-three-
    pence —
and turned out in the end to be selling a cure-all in a silvery
    tube.
The lamb in a side-street struck his poses underneath his
    white roses,
and above all this gallimaufry of tawdry and pittoresque
the failed mélange of architectural styles on its hill justified
    itself
by the great doorway and the two great windows.
Above the great doorway the stone is the colour of ivory.

Fireworks in Córdoba

Cocks and coins and golden lupins,
parachutes and parasols and shawls,
pamplinas, maltrantos, and glass lawyers,
giant spermatozoa, dwarf giants,
greengage palms, and flying goldfish,
comanche headgear filing up the water,
cocks and coins and golden lupins.

Combs and crowns and golden lupins,
assumptions of banderilleros in gold garb,
fantasies abruptly stopped like shot prey.
And the smallest boy hiding in his mother,
and the old men calling for castles and
not getting them; and on the Roman bridge
over the Guadalquivir spatchcocked Raphael
turns an indigo back on men and fire;
his petrine envy perilous like fur.

Rubén Darío in the Paseo Sagrera

Searching, in patios and cloisters,
in patios owned by aristos
and clositers owned by monks,
I, that would gladly be rich but
contemn pride of line,
who doubt God and the tonsured doctors
who keep him lingering alive
in his iron lung,
but might not find it easy to refuse
if offered deification,
seaching in patios and cloisters
for beauty like a tourist for things about which
to say to his wife: 'C'est joli, ça!'
found, in the end, what I needed,
when from the red flowers toward the palm-trees
I saw butting up
in squat white stone
the unsparing likeness of an ugly man.

Palma de Mallorca

Hermance

The ageing maiden lady in the black beret and I
from the waiting tram watched with quiet faces
the workers by the roadside, one bare to the waist,
the other in a tight singlet with a taste for sweat.
In this country of men with blond hair and auburn skin.
They were ugly, burly and stupid-eyed, so
we turned away to read the parish news:
nouvel incendie criminel, un Suisse se tue aux Pyrénées.
Turned away from
the brutal summer native to their bodies.
The ageing maiden lady suddenly
moved out of myth and out of my
contemptuous understanding
when her man got in and sat beside her
with his black hair and pale strong face.

'Indian Lemon Linen,

That's the very thing for you,'
Kinsolving answered Eaglesome,
'that's what we will bring for you
late in the autumn when we come
back from Italy: far too late
for you to wear it here with great
comfort — which is, of course, the point:
you see — ' 'You need not force the point,'
Eaglesome cried, not much amused,
'I fear your plot for upside-downing
the ways of truth could be abused,
and lead your friends to frowning.

'I've heard of a smart shop engage
in Paris a poet as window-dresser:
and he put in a bird in a cage
and felt a cute and sage agressor
of all conformity because
the bird was made of metals, and
the cage of real bird feathers, claws
and beaks — easy to understand,
this put all Paris in a rage.
But then after a year had gone
and he still doggedly went on
with versions of the same bold game,
but weaker ones, the moment came
when friends rebelled against the flaws
in too perverse a truth and felt the laws
not merely of man but nature too
soiled by his persistent view.
So I'd rather not be over-amused
by your glib plan for upside-downing
the truth; I fear you'll be abused
by some for short-wind clowning.'

Kinsolving came right back at him:
'The Spanish word spelt "sol" means sun,

the French word "sol" means ground,
and you'll not find the power of one
till the power of the other's found.
Or, not until you've tried in vain
to find the truth in other men
can your own self's truth come talking plain
out of its golden, festering den.'

'These hints are crumbs, but never food,'
Eaglesome cried in pain,
'you'll never reach exactitude
by digging caves in Spain.'

'I'll not, of course, be all that great,
but still suggest (an earnest clown
remembering anarchies of love and hate)
the truth is upside down.
And I will wear a gown of thorn,
and a mask of crystal,
and stand on my head in the town of scorn,
and fire — '
   ' — a water-gun?'

Be Born a Saint

for Claude Tarnaud and Henriette de Champrel

Be born a saint; or keep,
as natural and faithful as your nails,
a retinue of calm conformities,
and social artifice: both minor, and enough
to keep the prophets of the great hypocrisies
from rice-bowl-breaking, and from breaking
your glasses, or your fall —
or inviting you in only as a good turn,
something like a bragitóir, your most grim
bousingot imprecation indulgently laughed 'with',
your lightest nonsense owlishly revered.

Be born a saint: with private means; or keep
some social graces, though society
appears ungracious; hating and noli-me-tangere
will seldom get you hated, but regarded
as an Untouchable — or an intangible —
oftener than you know, if less than you imagine;
when some rare force,
hateless, eager, and unhateable,
arrives and offers — by that time response
may be impossible, almost atrophied, a helpless
vaginismus, too slow. Unless, of course, you
become the bragitóir gone berserk, become literal:
burn down the Bourse, assault the Minister
of Picot-Edging in their brand of fact,
not only the kind in your own mind and poem.

Be born a saint; or keep
some calm irrelevant conformities: or else
love will take a turn for the worse
with every noble and ideally sensible refusal
to accept the loan of a tie from the cloakroom attendant,
with every wine-gum sucked furtively
all through Vexilla Regis,

with every pompous cliché in defence of love.
That's unattractive advice
from slow-learnt cowardice.

Failures in bravery are often listless: that learning
can hardly set me scrabbling in the glory-hole
for a greening evening-suit one size too large
the Minister of Civilization gave me years
before I disliked anyone; easier to wait,
beside the bed of delicately dying love,
for a typhoon or amazing medicine.
Love takes a long and garrulous time to die.

Driscoll in Paris

for P J Kavanagh

The second time Driscoll visited Paris, he was walking one day along the quieter reaches of the Rue Monsieur-le-Prince. Feeling depressed. But his heart lifted when he saw two small, dirty, ragged girls playing in the gutter outside a dingy bar: one was black, one was white.

Driscoll went into the bar to celebrate and record this.

Later that evening he found himself in the Place Alphonse Deauville, needing a leak. He entered the tin contraption in the centre of the square, and what did he see on the wall but these words: 'Mort aux noirs, comme aux juifs.'

In bed that night, distracted for once from the vast self-pity that usually crowded into his small room at such hours, he said aloud: Celui qui hait écrit sur les murs. I should have written that on the tin wall, he thought. Then decided that to cheer himself up he would saunter next morning in the sunlight up the Boulevard St Michel, where the faces are of so many colours, and so many of such beauty.

By eleven a.m. he'd walked twice both up and down that boulevard. From waking, he'd again been depressed by personal thoughts totally unconnected with De-wit-man-moet-baas-bly, and all those lovely contours of so many colours had failed to cheer him. He crossed the bridge and went along the Seine towards Concorde.

It was about five paces from the Pont des Arts that for one grotesque second his worry was interrupted by a fierce fanatical resentment against there being so many non-Europeans to be seen along the Boulevard St Michel.

Not even sleeping with a gentle enough Senegalese, which he did the following night, could ever delude Driscoll into claiming that it was not really Driscoll who had felt that moment of resentment. A moment that haunted and shamed him as long as he lived.

This Country

for Folke and Bernice Isaksson

Lagarto, chameleon, cicada:
exotic names for ordinary creatures,
but not exotic but the truest name
for the quick lizard's green flame,
and for untiring insects' drumming muscles,
and a glazed grey climber on a brown-gold arm.

Cicada, chameleon, lagarto:
exotic names have come to mean
more than exotic creatures: they mean Spain:
a youthful healing of some northern shame,
a southern place that happened to be Spain,
which then, its callower use outgrown, became
a real place, that could be loved and hated,
half-understood, abused, accepted, left.
A liberation from green fields,
but then their explanation, and their praise;
triumphant proof, to anger, The World Is Wide —
and then, the triumph calmed, is wide enough
to compass narrow islands in its love.

Chameleon, lagarto, cicada:
exotic names to say
'cette contrée
de moi que j'ai nommée l'Espagne': but now
to claim both ordinary men
gathering seaweed (ploughing the rocks of Bawn)
and ordinary men who trample wine
('con el alba', ploughing the rocks of dawn,
to plant some stubborn strength against
blind, brilliant plants of pride, or southern shame):
chameleon, cicada,
linking them, for all they know;
and sundering, against our grain.
Chameleon, cicada, yellow bittern:

meaning freedom, knowledge, but also Spain.
Exotic names long grown
familiar as a native grain:
adding their own special, bright, bitter fruits
to an only less ephemeral taste for roots:

Until the barren rocks of a lasting dawn
break us, like bird or crop or small green dragon.

Korea

Lemon tea, peanut butter, and cinnamon toast.
Then, at two in the morning, we left the pleasant room.
Liquorless, gay, and perfect, we sang down Merrion Row.
It seemed as if Rhonabwy's Age had come.

At Stephen's Green, for some reason, we bought a paper.
The scare headlines persuaded us we and all men had lost.
In a snack-bar, scared, we drank rat-coloured coffee.
After lemon tea, peanut butter, and cinnamon toast.

Speaking for Some

for Maurice O'Dwyer

There is no time or place will give us
the full acceptance we demand.
All there can be is tacit tolerance
and that we must come to accept.

Or, their ignorance or condescension
may surprise us into mistakes:
and some of us, taking too much for granted,
growing grateful, may lose our heads.

The clique-joke for once too shrilled in public,
the wrong ring worn on the wrong hand,
may not only harshen the voice of patience
but cause a franker fist to clench.

Exotic dangers — but could be more so,
and those who never take them kill;
there's little enough dignity in defiance
but none at all in full disguise.

If it were absolute, our indignation,
we'd not be men, but Greek gods.
To accept and use is not to worship,
and some just men make good their trust.

The fountain's tense and gay, balancing
an alloyed crown, like freedom, high.
And when it's dry, all glitter hidden,
it must feel soiled, rested, sly.

Look, No Hands

for Ernie Hughes

> *Lengua sin manos, cuemo osas fablar?*
> — Poema del Cid

I blame old women for buying paper roses,
yet pluck a dandelion: by the time
it reaches my lapel it's turned to paper.

I hate the winter, and blame drinkers
for hiding in dark pubs when the sun shines outside,
and could be enjoyed at sidewalk tables;
yet every time I visit a crowded beach
I bring a sun-ray lamp along.

I praise trust above all,
yet cannot let a friend post a letter
in case he might stop on the way for a drink.

I admire a stone for its hardness,
resembling it only in barrenness;
admire a butterfly's brightness,
resembling it only in brittleness.

I like speed, summer, the country roads,
but never could master a bike.
Believing in God because of the need to praise —
though fear alone, so far, makes me long to pray —
if granted another hundred years
I might learn
                how to say prayers.

A Tree Absolving

A small cherry in full flower
at a neo-gothic church door
suddenly breaks open all this
terrible dominical dreariness:
each young man defaced and lost
in that convict garb, Sunday best;
each girl's great hair clamped in a hat
shaped like a segment of tinned fruit.
But passing I stopped for a long look
at the tree, and the whole ban broke.

The undeniably elegant spire,
not wounding or climbing the air
so much as resting on it, led
up to the undeniable good:
the broad blue sun.
Max Jacob described the sun
as a pagan afraid to come in
to churches, but then the sun
locks no cut fruit in a coy tin.
I stayed out, like sun and tree —
like in that only, in that only —
and suddenly no longer had to try
against such granite odds, the cowed
passion of the Sunday crowd,
to feel the earth can be like heaven,
though hell is hallowed once in seven.

Fleadh Cheoil

Subtle capering on a simple thought,
the vindicated music soaring out
each other door in a mean twisting main street,
flute-player, fiddler and penny-whistler
concentrating on one sense only
such a wild elegance of energy gay and sad
few clouds of lust or vanity could form;
the mind kept cool, the heart kept warm;
therein the miracle, three days and nights
so many dances played and so much drinking done,
so many voices raised in singing but none
in anger nor any fist in harm —
Saint Patrick's Day in Cambridge Circus might
have been some other nation's trough of shame.

Hotel-back-room, pub-snug, and large open lounges
made the mean street like a Latin fête,
music for once taking all harm out —
from even the bunting's pathetic blunderings,
and the many mean publicans making money fast,
hand over fat fist, pouring the flat
western porter from black-chipped white enamel,
Dervorgilla's penitent chapel
crumbling arch archaic but east,
only music now releasing her people
like Sweeney's cousins on a branch unable
to find his words, but using music
for all articulateness.

But still the shabby county-town was full,
en fête; on fire with peace — for all
the black-and-white contortionists bred
from black and white enamel ever said.
From Easter Snow and Scartaglin
the men with nimble fingers came
in dowdy Sunday suits,
from Kirkintilloch and Ladbroke Grove came back

in flashy ties and frumpish hats,
to play an ancient music, make it new.
A stranger manner of telling than words can do,
a strange manner, both less and more than words or Bach,
but like, that Whitsuntide, stained-glass in summer,
high noon, rose window, Benedictbeuern pleasure,
and Seán Ó Neachtain's loving singing wood,
an Nollaig sa tSamhradh.

Owls and eagles, clerks and navvies,
ex-British Tommies in drab civvies,
and glorious-patriots whose wild black brindled hair
stood up for the trench-coats they had no need to wear
that tranquil carnival weekend,
when all the boastful maladies got cured —
the faction-fighting magniloquence,
devoid of charity or amorous sense,
the sun-shunning pubs, the trips to Knock.

One said to me: 'There's heart in that,'
pointing at: a thick-set man of middle age,
a thick red drinker's face,
and eyes as bright as good stained-glass,
who played on and on and on
a cheap tin-whistle, as if no race
for petty honours had ever come to pass
on earth, or his race to a stale pass;
tapping one black boot on a white flag,
and us crowding, craning, in at the door,
gaining, and storing up, the heart in that.
With him a boy about eighteen,
tall and thin, but, easy to be seen.
Clare still written all over him
despite his eighteen months among the trim
scaffoldings and grim digs of England;
resting his own tin-whistle for his mentor's riff,
pushing back, with a big red hand, the dank mousy quiff,

turning to me to say, 'You know what I think of it,
over there?
          Over there, you're free.'
Repeating the word 'free', as gay and sad as his music,
repeating the word, the large bright eyes convinced
of what the red mouth said, convinced beyond
shaming or furtiveness, a thousand preachers,
mothers and leader-writers wasting their breath
on the sweet, foggy, distant-city air.
Then he went on playing as if there never were
either a famed injustice or a parish glare.

                                        Ennis

Refusals

for Benedict Ryan

The bus poised a-crest the bridge —
a traffic-light severe — some passengers
turned, waiting, from watching red sandstone
and cool green copper on the town-hall tower,
and looking right or left grasped a brief glance
at nature's light so grudging this late autumn
on the blue calm water in the Grand Canal;
that halt by water and its unsurpassed
capacity to welcome light consoling,
like many times in other broken weathers,
for stone-trapped Richmond Street and Rathmines Road.

But now the lookers-right saw only light on water —
leading to patriot-plaque and playing-pitch,
and purchase-homes in acres of slum-clearance —
while we who turned our rain-soiled eyesight left,
towards Ultan's hospital, the sunlit babies,
the locks where boys would bathe in better summers,
the film-censor's office, and green trees down
the Leeson-Baggot vista proud as Europe,
saw the familiar barge not level-changing
but stopped (they never stop), and a man bending
in soiled white overalls from blunted prow
to root with a long stick among the reeds,
half-heartedly encouraged by three boys,
his back to the hoarse hoardings, no swans breeding;
and as the red light ambered into green
I grew so curious about him
I felt I must get off and watch
till he found whatever he was seeking;
though even then I mightn't have been able
to tell what he'd found, and certainly
would not have dared to shout down from the bridge,
before those three brash gawpers, to enquire.

So gazing back till houses killed the view,
and one behind me thought I wanted her,
I rode on homeward half-an-hour too early
for lunch, and realized,
watching for six more stops the head in front,
it owned the first bald patch I'd ever noticed
with dandruff round the edge; and feared that feeling
had come too close to utterance,
the way the man just then looked out, back, down,
his nose grazing the window, his eye mine,
as young and old may do from pleasanter motives.

I rode on homeward, feeling well defeated,
I should have clambered down at the traffic-lights
to watch the man poking among the reeds:
to keep down curiosity seemed as grim
a crime, that day, as rancid a refusal
as when, last year, the girl in front
(met five years earlier) turned half-round,
glanced briefly, smiled briefly, and I —
got off three stops too early, knowing fear
too sensible for her
twenty-three years and yellow hair. That famous
Bolivian-Indian bracelet of beaten silver
still clasped her brown-gold arm, but could not force,
for all its magic glitter, better than refusal
out of me: no more than could
a long, unpolished, grey-black stick
searching the reeds that verge a dying canal.

A True Story of the Class War

A messenger-boy from near Ringsend
    came cycling up Clyde Road,
where all the Chevs are shining
    and all the lawns are mowed.
The boy was singing raucously,
    the sun was in the sky,
the blue was almost Latin blue
    and even keeping dry.

When down the path a proud young prince
    came skipping plump and gay,
his Conleth's cap upon his head
    was drunk with holiday;
and many might admire his curls
    and the youth and joy he showed —
but not that sweating working-boy:
    in summer, in Clyde Road.

The Prince of Conleth's, unaware
    of czardoms overthrown,
went blithely onward relishing
    his velvet ice-cream cone.
Perhaps his mind was relishing
    some classless boyish dream —
but all his tongue was seen to do
    was lick that huge ice-cream.

So Ringsend swerved his bike across
    the burghers' tar-bright road —
with hunger as his heritage,
    and cruelty *his* code.
Then drawing skill from dynasties
    of Guinness-drinking sires,
he spat into the pure white joy
    that every boy desires.

And rode off on his errands, still
    underpaid, but proud —
as much as if he'd killed a king
    or tommy-gunned a crowd.
Now that was a noxious, vicious child,
    as petty as they come:
but who's to know when he grows up
    which danger he'll become?

The story, though it's ugly, had
    an end that could be worse:
for the young prince had a sister,
    and the sister had a purse;
and though she knew no cash could clean
    or win back that foul price,
it still could take a small boy out
    and buy another ice.

Stephen's Green

A man walked past me in Stephen's Green,
amazing how like me he was:
just the same height, the same build,
wearing, like me, a grey-green gabardine,
wearing, like me, glasses,
bearing, like me, books,
his lower lip, like mine, large —
and there's the difference:
I reckon his might be firm,
not loose like mine.
For he's what is called black,
and I'm — take a look in that mirror —
what is often called white.
How long can he like this burg
where the glic may call you
'pathological'
for challenging words like
'nigger'?

Or should we wear yellow this winter?

Ballad

On Sunday as elders came out of the church,
leaving both lovers and pence in the lurch,
three young girls played hopscotch with a type-ribbon tin,
and the sunlight came out and the sunlight went in.

On Sunday as elders came away from the church,
or lingered to gossip in front of the porch,
three small girls played hopscotch with a type-ribbon tin,
and the weather was winter, but it seemed they had fun.

That morning I'd neither a lover nor pence,
but who that's had either could ever see sense
in leaving love's blankets till the pubs opened up
and we could walk forth for the loving black cup.

That morning as elders said prayers or felt cold,
and in warm foreign cities good drink was being sold,
three children played hopscotch with a type-ribbon tin,
and maybe they'll lose love, but maybe they'll win.

Men's Mission

Some Lenten evening sharp, at five to eight,
pick a suburban road both long and straight
and leading — which do not? — to a Catholic church:
you'll see, whisked out through every creaking gate,
men only, walking all at the same brisk rate,
    all in the same direction,
    with never a defection,
towards a certainty that needs no search,
to put the women in the ha'penny place —
as well they can, being not of Latin race.

If you could stroll the centre of the road —
you can't, the rich come too, the Gaelic god
indulges Lutheran cars but never Venice —
you'd see this ancient, muddled, rigid code
compose to symmetry a seldom ode:
    on left as right, the style
    of striding's Indian file,
the classic straight and narrow — leave to Venus
and her envoy, the wife, all curving now;
this week the gelding's sacred, not the cow.

Follow the dark backs, bent with Be-in-time,
into the church itself (you spare a dime);
as near the door as she could get, one last
pale woman kneels as though she prayed a crime —
to take up so much room at such a time —
    her face contracts — a skirt
    daring to gather dirt
from wooden boards! when trousers could stick fast
in hearty holiness to her very place,
or big plain hankies keep a crease in grace.

All city round, the week the men take over
the women's meeting-ground, and under cover
of black male skirts their slacker wives outdo,
the Venus breed, to visit their True Lover,

must unobtrude in porches, may font-hover
    (timid as drinkers in
    a Sunday pub at ten)
or traipse to distant priest and parish new,
like regular drinkers 'on the dry' for Lent
at mercy of curate strange, far foreign pint.

But here and now the Adams all are in,
'a truly magnificent congregation of min'
the old priest soothes before he launches out;
his sweet-voiced junior burks all talk of sin:
'Oh my dear men! Christ only longs to win
    your Friendship. He was A Man!
    Live up to Him! You CAN!'
then suddenly, bull-voiced, Man-voiced, lets a shout
you'd hear in hell, to wake a solitary ted,
and one old ashen pensioner, from the dead.

The ted glares all around him, dull defier;
the pensioner'd failed to see the amplifier
above the seat so nicely near the door;
the stolid rest sit on, the ladies' liar
flicks fidgets in them, soars, regardless, higher;
    then hymns: that curving Latin
    as only they can flatten,
and ('one verse now before ye go') 'Faith OF'
and OF and OF — but where's one sound of Love?

Phrases from Isaac of Nineveh

The tears of a man will flow
several times a day.
Then he'll come to continual tears,
and climb toward serenity.
All that is prayer stops,
and the soul prays outside prayer.
When the Spirit dwells in a man,
the man never stops praying,
for the Spirit prays always in him.
Asleep or awake,
his soul cannot lack prayer.
Eating,
      drinking,
            resting,
                  working,
drowsy:
spontaneous prayer shall perfume his soul.
He'll have no set time for prayer, but be
possessed by it continually.
Even given over
to an appearance of sleep,
prayer secretly invades him.
As a man drest in Christ puts it:
for people in serenity, silence is prayer.
Thoughts in a purified spirit
are like silent voices
praising, in secret, the Invisible.

Perfection

for Jonathan Gaine

The perfect creature I invented
on the fogged bus-window,
a five-stroke speleologic elegance,
more pleasure gave the moment
my index finger drew it
that Bach or Altamira,
or money, could confer,
or pretty people in the street;
but soon paled, appeared thin;
yet did not die
with expected speed;
at my halt, by the Garda barracks,
the bus lurching reluctantly
into the curb, suddenly
I wanted for some reason
to kill the perfect creature;
wondered, for seconds, why —
while the bus utterly stopped
and I thought: a further stage
would mean an extra penny
or abuse from the conductor
or, who knows, an inspector —
then rubbed a flat hand
over animal and fog
like any bored passenger
wanting to see some public clock
or pretty people passing in the street;
and rushed out of the seat
and halfway down the stairs
met someone coming up and
crushed past and barely made it,
leaping onto the path
into the Sergeant's arms;
and seldom again may draw
five such perfect strokes.

Friday in a Branch Post-Office

Sometimes I've to share a queue with old people.
I need stamps. They need money.
All the other stamp-hatches are closed.
And one of them after getting the shekels
kept us all waiting while she bought a stamp,
then of course she had to drop it on the floor
and the old man next in line, in front of me,
was peering down but clearly couldn't bend down
so I had to.
Have you ever tried to pick up a stamp off the floor?
'Postage of the Republic of Ireland
One Cent
The Fenians' —
why can't they send the money to them
instead of cluttering the stamp-queue?

But why can't they?
Why can't they?
Even young fingers are cold on winter mornings,
even young fingers may drop a stamp on a floor,
even old feet might stamp on a floor
with anger.
Old feet might need to walk out on a morning to feel
still with it but don't give me that crap:
if they sent the money to them they'd have more
summer mornings to walk out on summer mornings.

1867 it said on the stamp within a stamp.
Some of them looked nearly as old as that,
some must feel as old as that.
And one, behind me, had a white stick.
Old white sticks must need to grope forth on a winter
morning to feel still with it.
A hundred years: twice fifty —
and how many Masses can you leave for your soul
with One Cent?
With One Contributory

or Non-Contributory
Cent?

We don't need a statue of Cú Chulainn
in our Branch Post-Office.

1967

Texte établi

A woman took an emerald
out of her house
and laid it on the grass
and looked at it.
But nothing at all happened.
The green stone refused to look ashamed,
the still-shining stone remained
as bland as though it still, not sunlit grass,
could best cure poison.

The woman took one tuft
of grass, not soft
as a lawn may look, but coarse,
and stuffed it in
her jewel-box, but nothing much
happened, save extra work for maids. The coarse
grass refused to grant a bloodstone grace,
or wear its garb of glowing sun to such a gleaming
precious place.

From jewel as from blade
the woman made
one text: Refuse to change.
And wore it well.
She wore green rings to Mass,
and bathed upon the grass on fitting days.
Thought one day of planting jewels
next year instead of herbs, but, cautious, mean,
changeless, did not.

One day, grass-bathing, she forgot
an emerald ring
behind her on the grass
when dinner called.
When it was found, a green
grime in its tricky silver setting called
for soap. And she, for a second, watching

the ring froth, glanced, panic! at her finger:
but no, still slim —
Not yet a gross gloss on her thin text.

Sermon

Accustomed, long ago, to believe himself blind,
not only in mind, mark well, but in body as well,
he got a great surprise when, at last, un ciego manso,
mansísimo in fact, applied for his aid:
in crossing a quiet street:
he bore that cross like a crusade,
then found, when they had reached firm ground,
not only could he see, but even had quite forgotten
how not to. Briskly grateful, no longer manso,
firm as ground, the blind man walked off briskly,
tap-tapping smartly, leaving him standing there
feeling quite forgotten, needing a stick,
a naked white stick with a black knob carved
in the shape of a hand. The wall above the strand
was too naked a white, blinding his new sight,
his new eyes, he could not stand steady, feel safe,
without a stick to crack on some pavement's back,
on some black nightmare of a lost belief,
some dead bitterness proved unwarranted.

Spring

We like them so much on the branch,
green for heart's comfort, stoical copper-beech,
    and those pale sides that look aloof
but can be held and crumbled like any leaf.
    Now when they make us slip in lanes,
October colours by November rains
    corrupted, they get in the way
that's all, and by the ones that somehow stay
    aloft a short week longer we
are bored, waiting almost impatiently
    for bare black boughs we can call stark
or by less obvious names, which don't work
    as well as often as we'd like,
trees' truth, or strength, if any, staying stuck
    too stubborn inside wood, sap, air,
so outside us, not granting near-despair
    a lasting healing, not entering
our monstrous weakness, that eternal Spring.

Scour-proof

for Pat Broe

Some men invent a mask behind
which truth may celebrate, but they
wake one fine day to find
it's all the time been peeling
patchmeal
off.

I, slow to learn each man is born
to a thin, helpless mask, met fast
those glib planners with glib scorn;
till now, third-nature, scour-proof,
mine clings
thick.

[handwritten annotations, left margin:] their masks have been broken down—perhaps they feel they can expose true selves

[handwritten annotations, left margin:] His must Remain concrete & unbreachable

[handwritten annotation, bottom:] good poem to demonstrate the façade you have to retain in the face of homophobia, also other minorities

Distortions

What a surprise you got —
ageing yourself and using
sexagenarians calmly
as mirrors
not really distorting
but merely prophetic
and so much more reliable
than the glass in the bathroom
that gets the sun in the morning
or the one in the hall
that never gets any at all —
What a surprise you got
when one reliable mirror,
who knew himself 60 not 40
so could not need you as a mirror,
thought you were flesh not glass
human not mineral
and therefore unbreakable,
and not recognizing
himself as a mirror
in your extravagant sense
proceeded to treat you
like a toy, like a brother,
and though you were flesh not glass
you broke, and bled,
not sand or calcium either
nor dull red lead —
so how surprised you felt
assembling yourself on the pavement
flesh not glass
watching his creased nape
moving away, calmly,
as if it had never seen
itself in a flower, a child,
or another old man.

Power

for Soledad Pocaterra Thornton

Let the strong despise pity;
who needs it may not.

I've seen pity like a cul-d'jatte
reaching his powerful arms up
to steady a tall walker on trembling legs
and watch the walker move away,
come back to thank, then move away again.

I've seen pity like a basalt nipple
ancient women scrabble over in sand.

As no report of drowning
destroys the glory of swimming
or leaning over a stream-bank
to cup hands for drinking,
the sensible, the cautious can't kill pity.

For pity is only despised
by those whose pity despises.

Freakspiel

When you meet
your next freak,
be gentle with him, as always, but forget
to drive home,
as you drove
to that last one, so charming, so controlled,
how despite
normal spite,
his own ogling at the madhouse gate, he's yet
by his rare
gifts a fair
though marginal amusing member of the we-can-cope-
    with-it fold.

What freaks
you may meet,
in a world of you and them, want to be told
is not how
their bow
makes up for incurable wounds so ugly your
stomach boils;
no, dear pals,
that way only makes freaks more freakish, more
pure, what they
want you to speak
is very simple: 'You are as human as us, you are not a
    freak.'

For they, who at
that mad gate
cast only a flirting glance, caught from the prisoned cries
a new guilt
at their own filth,
an echo of cleanness in those soiled, jailed cries,
an awareness
in your nice

nappies of crap, as of cleanness in your tolerance —
oh clean,
dry on
the line, my dears, your hard-won, freakish tolerance.

Dear Gods

Dear God of Life,
give me the strength
to kill myself;
all you gave me
was life, and words:
the life so frail the words
blare to keep it going,
yet remain
weapons too weak,
sounds too hoarse,
to harm any, though
many pretend my words
hurt more than all their fists.

Dear God of Words,
who gave me the strength
to misuse words,
give me the strength
to use them well enough
to hurt myself as much
as those who claim my handless tongue
hurts their strong
mute hands, their proud
unspeaking speech,
eloquent stammer.

My hands of flame should reach
up to their violent tongues
and pluck them out and help
them and me at once;
but honesty's a rare flower,
speech is one of its fields,
honesty's a rare plant,
one of its claims: touch.

A word may call an action
brother but action seldom

answers back except with
back-of-the-hand mute strength.
Dear God of Strength,
give me the word;
if truly this butter-fingered tongue
has done such deep harm
to those who might have loved me,
whose only revenge is
silence, and absence,
and loving me without obsession,
and violence — breaking me
to break their own love —

Then give me at last the gentleness
to make one wild final scene,
fall silent, leave.

Dear God of Silence,
cut my tongue;
dear God of Absence,
come.

Dear God of Gentleness,
tell your twin
to give me his Violence
to kill myself;
only you
were worth serving;
I served him too much,
even if only by words:
he owes me, now, his aid.

From One Lover to Another

He won't let me name you.
He's talked about you so much
I even began to believe he believed me —
despite my endless monstrosities —
worthy of talking about you. But now,
he won't let me name you. So great his need was,
and must be still, to talk about you,
he seldom thought —
Christ! for one so taken to think at all
of such was noble, hard like ploughing rocks —
of how much I'd be hurt (nor able
always to hide that hurt
behind a shifting mask of real
interest and false interest) by
the simple, so natural act of naming you.
But naming you — what name? For he, stubborn,
warily ungenerous and with powerful cause rejects
the word 'love' and by not naming it
would escape its powerful fact. How then
could he link your name, so loved,
with love's name?
He's borne so many years the coarse weight
of my rancid affection
that even naming love may turn him brutal.
I suffer a selfish and futile suffering to think
by loving him I've helped him
hate love.

But nobody hates love.
Some think they hate it — at the shrillest moment
of pontificating against its name,
against its fact, they're in secret preparing
gentle actions, affections, proofs of stubborn love.
And so when he performed you in the theatre
of my curiosity and patience
(until the day I left before the interval),
naming you more often with every scene,

it soon grew clear how much it cost him to keep
from naming love. So your name grew to be
one of its other names, though he never resorted
to even the soberest lexicon, the most officially
humble, perhaps hypocritical imprecisions:
affection, warmth, friendship, all their blurred synonyms.
But he spoke like a man in love. He could no more
have kept from talking to me about you
than kissed me on the mouth in a crowded street.

So now in this quiet room, this mind, I risk your name.

from the author's own Castilian,
Barcelona, 1964

Clear Flowers

Symmetry after hot grotesque
a welcome thing, cool as a Cour des Myrtes
should be.

Naming the coast from Alassio westward
Riviera dei Fiori, the coast from Alassio east
Riviera delle Palme thus
                              making the city a pivot.
The beautiful balance of two streets in Milan:
one leading off to the right called Via dei Fiori Oscuri,
one to the left called Via
                              dei Fiori Chiari.
Charm of three-legged races, club-foot, private eye-patch:
undeniable, sad kenner. But now bizarrerie's
garlic breath begins to bore. Too like my own.
Cul-d'jatte may yet be me. Namur stilt-runners
could be ungainly as electronic carillons,
not all carillons dishonour quiet canals —
tall stilts, unfastened, could be placed,
identical, side by side,
symmetrical, smelling of mint.
Don't saw that stilt in two for a while yet,
dark urchin,
this Via could be
                              dei Fiori Chiari.
And I must hirple or trundle down it,
darken it somehow, piss on mint.
Though still I've seen the skies of Venice
through chinks in a low white arching
hill-field wall near Carna
and God or his brother in a flowering greengage tree.

Making Progress

Outside the madhouse gate, some lustra gone,
I stood, agog to get in. A madman fixed
came quickly carefully out. I begged him share
the wisdom and beauty he'd learnt there —
so bettter than our grim farce outside.
'I'm sane,' he glared, belting me half-up the drive.

Scuttling out, in the nick of time, I read the Marquis.
Like a failed saint kissing photos of lepers.

Chore

When you see what you are
hated,
when you see what you love
hated,
you may begin to hate
that hatred,
you may be tempted to hate
those enemies.
(An exiled Spanish Republican
cannot help hating
those who hated love
so much they destroyed it.)
For such temptation
I claim in those
who accept what they are
and may love you,
though not what you love,
understanding
and forgiveness.
Of those few lovers,
perhaps mythical super-beasts,
our no doubt failed redeemers,
who never hated,
I beg mercy.
When you feel human warmth
in those who claim to hate
but fail to act on it
you may fail to hate,
you may forgive,
because you need warmth,
and hatred's a hateful
tiring chore.
When you see what is real
though not your own
hated,
when you see what is real
and could be loved

73

hated,
you may begin —
though scorn spread false
claim to laughter, and pity
its pitiful, powerful charms —
to hate those enemies,
those mockers, messers,
those who've hated themselves
so much
they've almost no warmth left.
For love driven by hatred
into ghettoes I claim
release and, failing that,
some understanding,
which only the glib distrust.

hatred affects
the person
who hates

The Ba's up the Slates

for Toti Puig-Bo

For some, pin-ball machines, noise to keep out sound
of thought, feeling, fear, the try for love.
Noise to keep sound out,
keep silence out, that other silence keep
well in — it only lives in noise.
For many (gauchos gone, the bulls extinguished) foo'bol:
you can't play yourself but phone Di Stefano
to threaten death unless he score
90 goals tomorrow — or if he does.
And off to the great new stadium trot the proud Crusaders
of Sport, etc, cheap fat cigars
plugged in their gobs like soothers;
and, for a few, just roof-ball:
'the ball's still on the roof', a drunkard grinned,
tapsalteerie on a skinny stool,
'the ball teeters,' he roared, 'the proper state is bouncing
up and down, air/ground, ground/air, not slate-stuck,'
I'd asked: 'Roncalli dead yet?'
'La pelota está en el tejado todavía.'
But some, like me, play roof-ball day and night:
we're too slow and muddy for air,
too high-falutin' for ground:
moribund percht 'up' here, courage-bag bulged
with balance-panic, must pretend we know
all about thought, feeling, fear, love, sound,
music, silence, even noise . . .
Vertigo's, officially, antipodal; death we name
with fearsome trembling courage, often enough; and claim
that naming death we kill death.
                     Roof-ball,
puff-ball, blown, a summer second. One of these years
we'll tumble down at last; a curious child,
or insect, take the ball to bits, and find —

at best, some writing. Or a well-marinated tongue.
And the whole world in his hands, a globe of noise and —
'The ba's up the slates!' cry loud!

Spain 67

En todas partes he visto buena gente.
— Antonio Machado

Keep us ignorant for centuries,
generations, decades, we'll start getting born
stupid, the murder machine
works: young rebels
don't ever know how to rebel, our most
rebellious utterance clogged, unwitting,
with all the old doublethinks. A few
changes — the Republican school-books
quickly murdered, a grudging
tambourine tourist prosperity —
can only flow into the mind
slow, stemmed by our patience
(confusing with its opposite),
patience the old mask or ally of fear —
and we have reason to fear. And yet:

                            we
                            still
                            are.

Ignorance riding down ignorance,
no one listening to anyone else enough,
new press laws altering little,
crumbs of truth from the rich liar's table
flung to the cheated glaucoma'd heirs
of men who told themselves 'I've seen
good people everywhere,'
pre-signed referenda,
all those paper façades
of schools and hospitals camera'd fanfares opened,
empty of desks, children, beds, sufferers,
the children learning other things elsewhere,
the sufferers suffering still — hearing?

                            someone singing,
                            not flamenco.

Still as before
impossible to pick up a paper
without the familiar faces, the incomparable
cynical names incurable streaming out
like roaches from a kitchen wall.

Noise and Wind

Live in a foot-hill house, the wind
shrills down to kill; croucht
over ineffectual braziers,
washing by dangerous gas,
you find the world swell
to a vast whirl-wind,
you feel the world shrink
to a mad emptiness, wind.

>   Combs and empty hair-oil bottles
>   shoot the rapids dead;
>   the world's a pointless drama,
>   speed, chaos, dread.

Live on a thriving thoroughfare,
you can't sleep at night; crampt
under flimsy sheets; the traffic
makes such a hellish noise;
the whole world swells
to a gust, a globe, of noise;
the world's grown
a blown bag of noise.

>   Cloisters, verse, tranquility
>   drop dead;
>   the world's a pointless music,
>   storm, noise, dread.

Speaking to Some

You've seen hostility, ignorance, and fear
on many faces in every street; have seen
on attractive faces, kindly faces, on those
even more strange than yours,
laughter begin assassination
like tourist and christian trivia pinned up in the places of
    pleasure and worship
the Moors left in Andalusia;
watched, on ugly and stupid faces, laughter begin assassi-
    nation
like an incompetent erotic drawing scrawled on a latrine
    wall;
and watched the brilliant, watched the young,
abdicate youth and abdicate brilliance
when you passed, funnier than a Christie Minstrel but less
    to be indulged;
you've seen: a pleasant-looking family, sitting round in its
    front room
after dinner on a warm evening, the windows wide,
break off its noisy animation as if you carried a sign
    commanding silence,
and a spear, and wore war-paint, and were
ten feet high; and, in a broad street, of three men talking,
two with their backs to you, suddenly the third interrupt
the minute discussion of sport or sex
and, sure and coarse like steam-rollers, the four shoulders
    turning,
the hair often black the perhaps shapely head replaced by the
    white shapeless face of non-knowing;
and heard, after you've asked the way and been told,
with enormous courtesy and meticulous truth,
as you moved away the snigger bursting out like a fart;
heard mothers moistly bristling with all the insignia of
    being mothers
respectable in trams with shopping-bags and with children
    obviously born in wedlock

tell their young to look at the weirdie, with the same
   urgency as they might say: watch-the-birdie.
So:
imagine from the anitpathetic
hunchback in his chair
that soon hate will manage a miracle, open the eyes of the
   blind man
selling matches at the corner to let him join in the fun;
and after the organdy nudges
of the wedding-party framed in the gothic door
await the stares of the laughing cavaliers
from car-windows following the flowery hearse;
know that responding with scorn or anger would work as
   well as entreaty would,
as well as a spit or a paper-knife would to break down a
   handsome prison;
and never know for what they are the few the innocent
   admiring stares
of those too young for tact and too excited to look away
and too shy to approach; and never know
the interest of those few that avert their glance knowing
how quiet a word is tact for the need it means.
And listen with fear, in the midst of fear,
to the overtures of hate.

Questions

What fun figures, what glib contempt
they made, those fáinnetics,
bony old men in bonny kilts, embarrassing,
who'd speak bad French, worse Gaelic,
but never in a thousand years that Sassenach sin;
their chums in black skirts, with black leathers
pouncing pounding on desk-tops
frowning flouncing a patriot's duty at children —
yr Catty-Kizzum, or anti-Zion Protocols: sacred, sacred —
making a beautiful thing sound ugly —
making the language of Diarmuid and Deirdre
sound a language of tyrants and fools,
making the Comte Arnau, Queen Elisenda,
crawl on all hundreds, killing,
if any thing is sacred, what might become so.

In young reluctant ears, bullied, bellowed,
it came like that: bared of music
like a writer of words; a dried fountain
with small pale lizards
pretending to be chameleons
scurrying about on the concrete.

Mock those: well you may;
but listen have you lived where
you look behind before you dare
speak your own language?
Where mica's granite, piss wine?
Where later — hate as futile as it's fierce —
you've barely to glance at your neighbour before you dare
speak your own language?
Where one fine day, the gun smiles, and everyone rumours
    a thaw,
but next night, the gun kills, and all remember the law?
Walk down the street and have thrust in your hand by
a solemn youth like a pimp for a night-club
grey gestetnered screeds extorting

in your own language —
a crammer's malversion of your own language —
your duty is: forsake, dislearn, disown
your own language?
Go to jail for speaking it too clearly,
get beaten up for speaking it too clearly,
lose — worse, get (sub-thorn) — jobs, for speaking it
    nearly,
while eminent Abbots are called commies for speaking it
    fairly clearly
and sons of old friends are though honoured to buy you
    coffee
embarrassed because you speak it
at all:
your old friends brought them up, cute men,
believing it culchie-klatsch: now, though sons might differ,
lacking planes how learn to fly
or crutches, walk — so skilled, mis-schooled, at crawling.

Poor pale young lizards,
not even feigning chameleon —
just feigning Castilian . . . Have you lived
where foreign fools crawl on all fours, shrieking
'I'm flying!' — their wings made of their knowing
your language is not a language?
And other foreign fools crawl on all nowts, pouting
'I'm flying!' — their wings made of their patting —
interfering, dangerous — your all-but-severed head?
Have you lived where twenty-five years of war
are called 25 Years of Peace?
And called that in your own language, on hoardings, in
    your city?
Or sung hymns in prison, been told by warders:
'Sing in Christian!'
Sung in a chapel in your own tongue in your own town
to hear invaders, black-skirt-swingers,
pray aloud your blasphemy be pardoned?

Using your chapel to prey that in.
Tyrants and fools impose words like 'mine'.
Have you met the gaze
not of ignorance
but instructed hate?
Have you seen friends distorted,
driven to be phony martyrs,
because they loved this language
and could not bear it gelt?
So lost the quiet service they were doing it,
the quiet service they and their like could do,
for a loud ineffectual service, now grimly quieted?
Heard your language called
Dog's Tongue? By men?
Heard it called Shit,
in a church?

I watched an old man watching
sardana-dancing in St James's Square:
he stamped and jumped and screamed and thumped his
    stick on the stones:
'I'm not for Catalonia — I'm against Castile!'
Or, like another man I know,
who in his own house from his great height
having spoken long and suave about this coarse mistake
suddenly dropped on all fours and said
'This is what they want to make us do' . . .

Was he wrong, my dears? He went too far,
my rationals?
Have you had your tongue cut?

At times I think bad French.

Song for David White to Sing

remembering Woody Guthrie; listening to Joan Baez

An old man drinking with a young man,
   a young man enduring an old:
there are some joys about that story
   still need to be told.

A boy comes up to the city
   and meets a lonely man —
all who like to think the best
   may think as bad as they can.

(And I hope it gets them far.)

The old man knows the city,
   its ways to charm and kill,
the boy may see in the old man's eyes
   a young man waiting still.

And so they may make teachers
   and so they may make friends,
learning youth and learning age
   until the old man ends.

(Or somebody blows the boy up.)

Have you watched the two together,
   have you watched them true?
the old man shooting the young man down,
   the young man daring to?

You know how hard a thing it is
   to like — or even love?
How shy and envied all that young
   man and that old man have?

(But just listen to one of them talking about the other once
he's out the door . . . BUT listen true)

Gràcia, '65

A True Story of the Civil War

for Kate Ward

> *. . . llur guerra civil contra els gegants.*
> — Pere Quart: 'Infants'

On a bridge in the north
a well-clad child, alone,
playing with snow, caressing it.
Under the bridge flowed
a river of stone,
no water but street,
no water but snow.
Cold winter siesta hour,
snow-sleep, white fear.
In that false-young silence, the child held
to snow and rich clothing:
the snow his better wealth, for now.
And into that silence let fall
a sizeable ball of snow,
caressed, perfect, as white
as hot walls in the south.

Leaning on the snowed parapet
over the stone stream,
he watched in grave pleasure how it fell
far into silence, into the only eternity
(that of a child on his own).
I watched in pleasure that child in his grandeur,
watched from twenty yards
and a thousand years away
him sending the snow to get dirty
in stone, mud, ice.

There was nobody under the bridge.
The whole world slept.
A ball of snow fell
like cherries on silk,

like a green chiffon scarf falling . . .
but past me a furybound grown-up erupted
(green greatcoat ankle-deep,
glasses, unpardoning senescence): 'Das
ist nicht möglich,' striking fiercely:
he was a man, so he couldn't punish
the snow, the stone, his only hope
was hurt the child, the man in the child,
and the man who had died in himself.

So easy to hurt the good child
we never forgive in ourself.
He was a man: for him, the dirt
wasn't the stone or the cold mud,
but the white snow, the child's game.

The child went slowly away,
not saying a word, not crying,
caging his pain in the frightened silence,
in that grave pride they need.
I never struck the man, but watched him go
(he was even more ageing than I),
then leaned on the parapet
watching the river flow.

Prose

for Toni Turull

An anarchist poet in exile after the Spanish Civil War was asked by the University of Carácas to give a public course of poetry talks. He told them his fee was 2,000 dollars, to be paid complete the day before the first performance. They grudgingly agreed — he was truly an OK name.

When he got to Carácas, he demanded the money in single notes. To this, too, they agreed. He collected the paper in a suitcase borrowed for the purpose.

He then insisted his opening lecture take place really in public: not in some small hall where the people might be admitted could they find it, but in the main square of the city.

Heaven and earth were moved. So on the appointed morning the square was packed. Scholar-preambled, the Poet rose; and gazed down from the high platform, the height of his new capital P, over the morass of faces. Few of them looked any better fed than the ones he had seen in his own country, living under bridges in Triana, or in tin-and-paper shanty towns round cities. He remembered one thing in particular: the ragged bamboo palings enclosing a mud garden.

Listen, he said, they asked me to tell you about poetry. Well, I will.

He opened the suitcase and took out a note and held it up. A lovely crisp crackling thing, big enough to buy several platefuls of beans with, or pay the kitchenmaid for a month.

Does anybody want this? he asked. Many showed they did. He rolled it up into a tight ball and threw it down to them. They showed how much they did.

The anarchist glanced behind him quickly. The scholars, who admired his command of the hendecasyllable, had all fainted. He saw the crowd wanted more of this perfect poetry. So he took another note, and tearing it up flung the fragments to the people. Then he poured the whole suitcaseful down to them, one note in ten diligently torn into neat fragments (in his centrally heated hotel-room the night before).

Some young scholars, now, admire his work.

Nine Lines

4

And what I hope is: madness may not grow
beyond the gaudy height of eccentricity,
nor may the bravery for suicide
lend my lech for truth its rough duplicity.

3

When you write 'Love'
at the end of a card
be sure to make it illegible.

2

The power of love is great:
I have friends.

Ringing the changes on Mistral

My mother brought me forth to show,
the neighbours came and gave me

a couple of eggs,
a cut of bread,
a grain of salt,
and a match-stick,

telling me to be:

as full as an egg,
as good as bread,
wise like salt,
straight as a match.

And if I later became
as empty as a cracked eggshell,
as bad as bread gone green,
foolish as caked salt,
and pointless like a spent match,

recall, as in Paris partridge
is less than apples at home,
that once I may have been

egg-full,
bread-good
salt-wise,
match-straight.

Gaeltacht

for Liam Brady

Bartley Costello, eighty years old,
sat in his silver-grey tweeds on a kitchen chair,
at his door in Carraroe, the sea only yards away,
smoking a pipe, with a pint of porter beside his boot:
'For the past twenty years I've eaten nothing only
periwinkles, my own hands got them off those rocks.
You're a quarter my age, if you'd stick to winkles
you'd live as long as me, and keep as spry.'

In the Liverpool Bar, at the North Wall,
on his way to join his children over there,
an old man looked at me, then down at his pint
of rich Dublin stout. He pointed at the black glass:
'Is lú í an Ghaeilge ná an t-uisce sa ngloine sin.'

Beartla Confhaola, prime of his manhood,
driving between the redweed and the rock-fields,
driving through the sunny treeless quartz glory of Carna,
answered the foreigners' glib pity, pointing at the
small black cows: 'You won't get finer anywhere
than those black porry cattle.' In a pub near there,
one of the locals finally spoke to the townie:
'Labhraim le stráinséiri. Creidim gur chóir bheith
ag labhairt le stráinséirí.' Proud as a man who'd claim:
'I made an orchard of a rock-field,
bougainvillea clamber my turf-ricks.'

A Dublin tourist on a red-quarter strand
hunting firewood found the ruins of a boat,
started breaking the struts out — an old man came,
he shook his head and said:
'Áá, a mhac: ná bí ag briseadh báid.'

The low walls of rock-fields in the west
are a beautiful clean whitegrey. There are chinks between

the neat stones to let the wind through safe,
you can see the blue sun through them.
But coming eastward in the same county,
the walls grow higher, darkgrey:
an ugly grey. And the chinks disappear:
through those walls you can see nothing.

Then at last you come to the city,
beautiful with salmon basking becalmed black below
a bridge over the pale-green Corrib; and ugly
with many shopkeepers looking down on men like
Bartley Costello and Beartla Confhaola because they
speak in Irish, eat periwinkles, keep
small black porry cattle, and on us
because we are strangers.

Quinze juillet, early morning

A woman walking swiftly
along a moving barge,
an earthen-coloured crane
eternally revolving,
the big sand-coloured stones
dropping like jewels on the off-white stone,
the woman walking swiftly to the prow.

The private victory at quiet tables
over the slightly disappointing festival,
a half-misguided longing
for warm food and lovers,
the quai petering out in a cluttered desert
of trees and railings, iron rails and trains.

The sun between the trees, the momentary cold,
the coloured night as if it had not been;
a poem, like a breast, firming swiftly
under a quiet, an excited hand.

Seán O'Sullivan

for Carl Ordonez

He passed out in the pub.
People he may have thought
were friends began to talk about him;
not kindly. (Perhaps they
were friends.)
After a time he woke up,
stood up
to his great height, glared
down at them,
down;
and said, not raucous but emphatic
(echoing round the weekday afternoon):
'Ceapann sibh go bhfuilim as mo mheabhair.'
Then he sat down again,
and passed out again.

Few men ever had
more beautiful Gaelic, a richer voice.

And in a different pub, one day he was more or less sober,
and I was drunk, and under trouble
from the savages
(not the ones in me
but the others, their quislings),
he spoke to me kindly.
Amid savagery so deep
I dare not name it.
That single brief kind sentence held
more courage, more sadness, and grace
than most men manage in a lifetime.

So for him, who was not called my friend
but called an acquaintance,
I keep the kind thought waving

its three inverted commas
round about wildly
somewhere inside my barbarity.

Secret

They made an idol of this man, because
he did not have to break any to prove
there were none. But that was what he did
prove: that there were no idols.
So they made an idol of him.

They shouted subtle maudlinities about
his lack of sentimentality.
They wept happy cataracts of words,
frozen as melting snow, hard as turkish
delight, about his granite eye.

In this way, it remains a dowdy secret
that only his earth-sized, meticulous capacity
for admiration keeps him free of idols;
and the granite glory of his unrelenting eye
could not have been reared and lit by anything but love.

Lyde

tibi,
with corni da caccia

In the summer morning when I awake at six
   from crisp green sheets and blue, clear-headed after cider,
a squirrel is playing on the grass gently sloping
   down from house to brook. Dark, tough-looking birds
     jabbing
at bread left out in a long tin on a low table;
   rusty baking-dish on broken brown marble, a feeding.
The flowers near the brook's edge not doing so well:
   deer come out of the trees at dawn to eat the heads,
leaving only their footprints. I trot, clear-headed,
   across the dew to inspect the prints but cannot,
rude suburban, find them (school never toyed with nature).
   Creaking back through glass doors, easily find the pottle,
relieved a little still left, relieved it's only a little,
   not enough to be sozzled by mid-morning: enough
to drink slow, but not mingily, two long glasses
   watching the morning grow: squirrels, birds, a rumour
of antlers back there, somewhere, in the dense woods for
   a thrill — easy? cheap? Things ought to be easy and cheap
once in a while, even often, like this peace here
   given to me by friends, watching the sun make over
the long narrow water, the trees — I name those I know:
   beech, alder, ash, elm (All vowels alliterate),
I must ask my friend the name of the other trees,
   I'll ask him when the child awakes and is fed, when
the grown-up breakfasts are taken, the flower-heads tied
   in fishing-net against the deer — for soon we leave,
three for Italy, one for Bristol: exciting
   places! and so they are. But for me peace here now
is more than excitement, so between six and eight
   on a July morning I nurse the yellowish drink,
the green and blue nylon sheets, the Gloucester sunlight,
   the creatures. Feel gratitude (my own: not imposed),
mean love (perhaps could make it mine), one brief dry retch

of envy (that's mine for sure), then relax. Relax
at last. No shame, here, yet, for taking some peace.
What else do the starving and the tortured want?
Bread in a baking-tin, sun upon brown, a feeding

Sadlers Farm

Shaped like the bearskin on a guardsman's head,
with, in the top right corner, a slight dent,
the vast sycamore makes a one-tree forest
in the hollow between two grassy hillocks.
A field away, it fills my attic window,
and on this almost windless day no stir
of leaves can I detect, unless perhaps
near the centre where a little blue comes clear.
No trunk is seen, no twigs, no wood: all is green
except that saving patch of distant blue.
From the hollow the tree rises compact
like a crannóg from a Leinster lake.

Seen from elsewhere, some distance to the left
and lower down: from a green seat — Italian
plastic, the kind you blow up — the sycamore's
unique massive impact is part-concealed
by a leafless derelict-looking apple-tree
and eight black-and-white cows, chewing standing up.

Resentful of these obscuring things, I leave
down beer and book, and cross the grass, and climb
the white ladder to the white attic, to place
the sycamore back inside its right frame,
that small but perfect window. A maroon moth,
light-lured last night, seemed, on entering,
to fill my attic window, so that now
sycamore and moth make a full day.

Cotswold Nightflower

A bright flower in a cold night
implies a glow, the dandelion
recalls a yellow fire,
illusive warmth breaks through
the huddling sheets, keeps out
the howling wind scouring house
and ground — the yellow beak
of a blackbird pecking blizzard grass.

Poem with Justin for Paul and Nessa

Paul you brought us in
Nessa said Come to us

At three in the morning she said
Come to us
At four in the morning
you opened your door to us

At three in the morning
by four broken phones
by one phone that worked
by two lucky sixpenny bits
by five cruising taxis who turned us away
by one taxi that took us
by two bloodsoaked hankies
dropt on the nightmare street
by a long desolate street
by fear of pursuers to finish the job
we didn't know which way to turn
we didn't know which way led to you
at four in the morning
by grace of friendship
by grace of poetry
by grace of marriage
we came to you

We came home to you Paul
Nessa we came homing
Sara / Síafra
did we wake you up?
We came home

By grace of electricity
by grace of petrol
by grace of greed
by grace of money
we crossed London

When we got to your gate
your window was lit
you were standing there already
in the lighted doorway
at the open door
at the OPEN door

You brought us in you looked after us
you gave us a drink and a place to sleep
you listened

You washed my face gently
you washed the blood from swelling flesh

At three in the morning
in the terrifying city
well within hearing of the beast
by four broken phones
by two lucky sixpenny bits
by two red hankies
by the rending pain of coughing through beaten ribs
by the broken sleeping of two small children
by the strength of two tired people
not too tired
we came to you

Out of despair
onto a skellig of hope

Oh it was difficult landing
but you made it easy
out of your difficulty
we had it easy

Whatever blood whatever grime
I snuffle stumble blubber through
from now till the bloodstained hanky

drops in my nightmare street
I'll get washed in memory clean
made whole again
by Nessa telling us Come
by Paul standing waiting
at the lighted open door.

october/november '70
london-dublin

Into their true gentleness

for Katherine Kavanagh

If love is the greatest reality,
and I believe it is,
the gentle are more real
than the violent or than
those like me who
hate violence,
long for gentleness,
but never in our own act
achieve true gentleness.
We fall in love with people
we consider gentle,
we love them violently
for their gentleness,
so violently we drive
them to violence,
for our gentleness
is less real
than their breaking patience,
so falsely we accuse
them of being false.

But with any luck,
time half-opens our eyes
to at least a hundredth
part of our absurdity,
and lets them travel back,
released from us,
into their true gentleness,
even with us.

Geneva

for Bob Welch

The silver curving fish
upon the shining florin

Bent nearly double as they leant
over the parapet small boys
with home-made tackle caught
in as many minutes five
little silver shining fish
out of the green Rhone.

The silver curving salmon
upon the shining florin

The naked stone horsemen
proud on their tall pediments
flanked the long broad bridge
I watched the intent
excited anglers

An old man with a brown bald head
cried encouragement
and one of the boys who wore
a blue-and-white cap
crimson-tasselled
and clean white socks
crowed non-stop
in a shrill voice:
O ma petite
as the little fish came
swirling up on the line
lost for ever
to the clean green water
O ma petite, ma petite

Mama Poule

Mama Poule, as few called him, was invited to a party. Before the invitation was confirmed he had to pass through many tests, of a rigour comparable to those undergone in ancient Ireland by candidates for the Fianna, to prove himself for real. In the end he scraped through, and the party was unbelievably beautiful. So after that he went to many such, in various parts of this gob of laughter. But one night, on his way to one of these shindigs, he met in the street a girl he'd been at co-ed school with, a nice harmless girl who thought she liked camp. They hadn't seen each other for a decade, she told him she'd just come back from Athos, and suddenly a great nostalgic tenderness billowed up inside him and he asked her along to the party — knowing full well that, unlike Athos, no women were allowed; but hoping for once that ghettoes might be kinder than laws and customs.

Needless to say, they were both booted down the front steps at sight, by a hearty disguised as a non-hearty. Mama Poule saw the girl to a taxi (as usual, the last bus had just gone) and walked around in the somnolescent city, to see could he sober up and quieten down. He could not. So feeling closer to despair than ever before, even in the proudest quagmires of romantic love, he went to a sheebeen where he drank a great deal of bad whiskey out of coffee-cups.

He woke on a bench in Parnell Square, his arm round a sleeping whore. As dawn was breaking he saw that she had no nose. He left her there, and boarded the next plane for Granada, where he spent a long time trying in vain to kill pigeons in the public squares.

Not Clegs but Nightmares

When Franco's imperial crusaders,
puffing up their merkined nobilities,
having pacified Pamplona
a cristazos limpios,
reconquered Catalunya, Durruti
was already dead and buried. Thwarted
they refused to be thwarted but dug
'Durruti' up, tied his corpse to
a tree and a firing-squad
shot the corpse dead.

When Vassili Nikiforovich Chadayev
was killed by hired guns beside a road in
the Kuban his friends would have waked him
in Leningrad, the city he loved,
for he'd fought in the Rising of '17.
But this was not allowed:
he'd been exorcized from the Party:
a stone, with an inscription,
built on the spot where he died,
was broken into smithereens.

When some human beings fled Belfast
through menace in the holocaust
August of '71
they were stoned in the station as they waited
for a train down to comparative peace,
to a lesser inferno. These
are not yet utterly killed. But what more
did those dead stones need?
Or dream to breed? In vain?

Ireland 1970 Bolivia Year of Our Lords the Colonels Glasses Glinting

for Pere Quart

We've seen
a golden spine,
the twin birth of pine-needles,
riverbanks yellow with oranges,
the brightblue, tumbling Clady,
dawn down a valley.
We've been
to Amadora, Pnom-Penh,
Baggot Street Bridge, Athy.
We've known
a man worth more than his work.
We've dreamt
a man who never said mine.

We listened
to Constantino Suasnavar
translating Carleton
from Gaelic into silence.
Tenderness became manhood,
even daily.
We listened
to a small stone face in a chapel
serene but gabbling
across time.

Green lizard. Red seaweed.
A man in prison
freed us with his music.
We sprang to Farandouri.
We built furze doors,
and ate shamrock on the run.
We played the tenora
and the penny-whistle.

We taught some policemen to read.

We've met men
who beat or even escaped
evil — even vengeance
and competition;
who saw vengeance in the mirror
and smashed the mirror — some
whose minds never even re-assembled
those broken bits of glass
dredged up from where they lay
drowned
kissing deep in despair.
People whose joy and skill
was so great, though small,
they did not need to compete.
Mourning, help, forgiveness:
have not entirely mocked us.
We've hungered, murdered, worked.
All we ask is to be left in peace
to wage our little wars.
Babies, because mortal.
Growing because dying.

Must we then be ruled
by men who talk and act
as if they'd never been
seen
known
or dreamt?

let alone listened;
or danced.

dublin 5/6 december 1970

Pub Song

for Macdara Woods

There was an old fiddler who stood in the street,
    charming the birds of the sunlight and snow;
and when he got pecked by the cold birds of rain
he thought it was time to go inside again,
    so he found him a hospital bed, and he'd go —
        in he'd go!

But first he thought best to make sure of some heat,
    so he paid a barkeep for a gold baby Power:
then propped up in his bed in the old public ward,
he opened the bottle he just could afford,
    for a nightcap, a comfort, a cure!

But what had the playful bold vintners been at
    only filled up his bottle with bright lemonade!
So the bright turned to dull, and the warm turned to cold,
there was grime on the heart, there was lead over gold,
    and the practical joke was well played —
        was ill made.

Meanwhile in the house of the parish priest,
    the publicans famished their fill:
there was lashin's of water and crusts at their feast —
ach níor bhlaiseadar Muire, 's ní fheaca siad Críost —
    but they joked with a hearty good will
        (make you ill)

Now they'd never have played such a prank on a priest
    or a man with a stake in society,
but a man who makes music's a tinker at best
in the eyes of the demon those blind fools caressed,
    and so a fair butt for their piety.

By a thousand blind tinkers may their tills all be fleeced,
    their decanters all filled up with piss;
may they get the constrictions and not be released,
ná mblaise siad ól is ná bhfeice siad Críost —
    oh Mary, their opposite, grant them the kiss!

Belfry-Hunting

for Eiléan Ní Chuilleanáin

'Hunting belfries, like belling stags,
with beaters, from coverts, with shotguns,
with bows and arrows, with all that is bestial
but in us redeemed for this inanimate stone
we bring alive by hunting it.

Some do it with butterfly-nets,
hunting belfries with butterfly-nets,
they claim to see the noble towers
veering and weaving, or resting with upright wings,
sun-heat of centuries vibrant in
the grey-gold silent stone — more musical
than any bell — as membraned wings
are sun-suffused a single season,
the grey-gold stone like insects
living on honey — '

                  'Fritillaries,
vanessas, brimstones, Ambrogio,
Sant Climent de Taüll, a hillside
over a church in a stag-melodious glen,
cicadas:
'a tremble of light in the leaves',
the green-gold close-cluster of parasol-
pines on a headland the boat coming into
Palma harbour in the early morning — '

                      'Prou!
Recostracullóns! We have no room, I tell you,
for tourists and postcards, or coy
self-acclamatory poems, our sport is ancient
but never permitted the fantasies of tapestries,
we're Muslim-bigoted against the figurative,
the Anti-Stone-Sport League will never know it
but what we hunt is peace, and that requires

tenacity, sobriety, and eyes
but not for pictures. And the lepidopterists,
although we indulge them as affiliates,
are not card-carrying members, little better
than you or those Cockney upstarts
in the West Country who glimpsing a belfry
start in a flurry across the road
would run it down for dinner, not knowing
a car-killed belfry has no proper clang.

We are the only serious ones:
with bows, arrows, guns,
we're hunting and poaching for peace.

The Jailing of Devlin

They're against her because they're men
who think men are better than women.
They're against her because they're old
and she's young.
They're against her because they fear death,
as anyone with any sense does,
and because their fear of death
does not mean a liking for life.
They're against her because they fear freedom,
which no one with any spirit does,
they confuse freedom
with chaos,
because they can't imagine, though she can,
a freedom free of chaos.
They're against her, I've little doubt,
because of her long hair and her short skirts.
Why should young women
not wear long hair
and short skirts?
Why should young women
not wear trousers?
Why should old men
in antiquated wigs
not wear short skirts?

28 June 1970
dublin

Ageing

As in convalescence,
cake tastes like bread
and bread like dust.
But this is no convalescence,
only a deepening malady.

Travel was adventure,
is now ordeal.
Arrival is all,
and even then . . .
Journeys cannot be faced
without a companion:
so too many journeys
remain unmade.

Once I knew I'd speak
all tongues, and visit
every continent.
Mexico is dying,
Rumanian still stuck
at lesson eight.

Sex needs long warning,
and even then . . .

A little adulation
from the young supplies
the needful deceit-zest
to go on dying.
Their generosity
turns mean in my mouth.

Shame at physical
blemishes dulls: I no longer
long to wear a yashmak.

I stole a march and you stole a coaster;
black to a bright room

I thought you were the water,
    I thought I was a barge:
we drank our health at every lock
    and chickpeas free of charge.

I knew you were a smoker,
    and I was cannabis:
if rozzers learn their lessons wrong,
    we can't go on like this.

I felt you were a finger,
    I felt I was a nail:
and if we keep on scratching hard
    we'll end up in the jail.

I knew you were a dancer,
    I hoped I was the dance:
if I keep on like this I'll end up
    reading 'True Romance'.

I thought you were a drinker,
    I thought I was a snug:
who ever heard the mantis die
    on a sheepskin rug?

I thought you were a boarding-house,
    and I was both the lodgers:
Rackrent came round, we left a note:
    'Fuck the begrudgers'.

I dreamt I was a nightmare,
    I dreamt you kept me sane:
I counted planets by drops of sweat
    on the fractured counterpane.

I dreamt you were like Easter,
    and I was like the tomb:
done was the battle on the dragon grey
so I stole a march and you stole a coaster
and by bush out of bourbon we both went back
    to rise in a sundark room.
(Rise and fall,
        fall and rise,
                rise and fall
                      in a sundark room)

A True Story

When the liberator loved humanity (for all the dictators were dead, like west britons in Ireland or crackers in Georgia), a writer was sent to jail for sleeping with his fellow-men. That was about the time all those like him were rounded up — except the few that escaped the ice-box — and marched through the city with *W* on their backs meaning *warm*.

His time done, the writer got out of jail and wrote a book, not about things like that. A lenient nation considered him purged of his warmth, so the book could be published. It even won a prize — the biggest prize a grateful nation confers.

When the day for giving the prize came round, they held a jamboree. And when the writer, so recently out of grace but now covered in glory, was called up to get his prize, the chairman who gave it to him was the judge who'd sent him to jail.

So the writer climbed onto the platform and, putting his arms around the chairman (or judge) in time-honoured civic-tepid style, he kissed him not in time-honoured tepid style on both cheeks but warm and full on the mouth. With a resounding smack.

Like Trees, like Islands

I kneel to fasten your shoes.
I kneel, creaking, clicking.
We seem near.
Blade, thong, buckle.
I know by which notch
takes easy entry
how swollen, how tired, how rested.
How near we seem — like trees, like islands.
Like trees on their neighbouring islands
that cannot uproot themselves and walk —
no kneeling fingers —
on water to meet. But moved
by an occasional strong wind
they touch branches, tangle, may even
break each other. As long
as life, the heart tholes.
They know, in a way then, how near
their islands are. Swap nests.
Trunk-tug is too strong
for any thong not to give soon.
The meeting lasts only a minute,
but these minutes recur,
and in that minute the trees congress
their different bird-song, squirrels, iguanas,
climbing, swarming, crawling life,
fruits and flowers if any.
They can even share lightning.

I kneel to fasten your shoes.
We seem near.

Connemara

for Luis Cardoza y Aragón

Much good may it do me to steal prayers from Isaac
of Nineveh; much good to recall one drunken summer
afternoon when a greengage-tree glowed like God;
much good, an infinitesimal white fish-bone
prised from my throat and gleaming in the penumbra
of a doctor's room and whiter
than any whiteness while the traffic roared,
the pulsing unbearable decibels of July sun,
outside the ajar shutters — for what does all that prayer
come down to now but mere fear.
                      I stand, Cois Fharraige, watching
two swans and four geese on grey water
under a grey sky, lichen black or mustard
on grey and rust-coloured rocks, by the roadside
a knee-high yellow pole with a red band at the top
luminous at night: there must be a prayer here
but all I can catch is fear: I pray, quite panic-stricken,
to God to keep my ageing, weakened bowels closed
until we reach a hotel, I writhe in ludicrosity, beseech
the cough not rack. Still fear, and worse than ever.
(The fear of decaying food in a widowed bachelor kitchen.)
I pray against barbed wire.

In kelp cormorant fuchsia foxglove country,
collies and black-faced cream-wooled sheep,
drystone walls at once darker and brighter after the rain,
the quartz gleaming whiter in the gloaming,
I name Ben Gorm, Blue Peak, tingling day-luminous blue
in the distance, green close-to at Leenaun, I name
Lough Doo, Black Lake, Málaga-blue in the distance, harsh
blackish near-to. There must be prayers here.
I whinge against the barbed wire
of disablement, panic.

Seborrhea, cellulitis, rumplefyke.
Amylozene, Grunovit, Kaopectate.
I throw a dandelion down into the green-brown
stream of a nameless waterfall,
I watch — the right, lovely sound for a lovely meaning —
the yellow flower swirl aside out of the current,
amid mild suds be calm.
                              I pluck and throw
a second one down, it drifts under the bridge
back towards the fall. Hirpling to the other side
I crane over, peer; the flower does not appear.
Am I praying? Offering? Perhaps I'm praying
a true prayer.

Under the conical menace of a Gothic mountain,
in these green fields I pray against barbed wire,
and never forget to take my pills.

Sometimes Feel

Like an old, wrecked sponge-diver leaking,
like a suit-of-armour leaking,
like a tree-stump leafing
after the shameful white has darkened over,
like an unwashed potato brutally cut,
the sickly off-white spattered
with dark patches of decay.

Homage to José Martí

The Spanish bishop covets
pillars for his altar:
in my church, on the hill,
elm is altar.

Floor is fern,
walls birch,
the light comes down
from the blue ceiling.

At night the bishop
goes out to sing;
he rides, in silence,
on a pine-kernel.

I sleep sound
on a stone bed;
a bee grazes my lips,
and in my body the world grows.

Tell the blind bishop,
the old bishop of Spain,
to come to my church
on the hill.

A Rose and a Book for Sant Jordi

Brave Galinsoga strode up the aisle,
pocket tyrant of a half-cowed country,
the only beautiful thing about him his name,
and called, as the people were singing to God in their own
    language,
what they were singing in
shit. Proud Galinsoga, the boss-man's countryman,
the overpaid hireling, the white-collar jackboot-in-office,
called the word loud and clear, over and again,
just as the people were learning, at last, again,
the almost-forgotten, almost-undreamt-of feeling of
    freedom to sing
to God in their own language.
He got as far as the altar-rails, and then they seized him
    and threw him out.
Next day both to his private mailbox and his editorial office
there came an avalanche of little gift-packets
neatly tied in pink or yellow ribbons
containing small turds,
it being the national day, the day of Sant Jordi,
and the custom having been and beginning to be again, a bit,
to sing to God in their own language,
on that day, their day.

Galinsoga: beautiful nine-letter name.

Ode to the Future

for Brian Lynch

How wrong, how stupid, to gibe
'living in the past':
the past is alive in us now.

When I order a Smithwick and pep,
and the rude barman, serving, says
'God that must make it taste awful!'
Croesus is boiling a lamb and a tortoise
in a bronze oracle-testing pot,
thousands of Spaniards are drinking, tricept,
thimbles of potent Pipermint,
a man called Josep, called dead —
oh truly dead, oh my darling Queralt,
far from your high native rock —
is saying to me, in his Perpinyà garden,
under the bees and the jet-planes,
over the wine and the pigeon-in-cabbage,
'he donat la meva vida al amor dels amics':
I gave my life to loving my friends.

When I gulp coddle, the bacon tender, the milk tough,
with a tough, tender, young widow,
Peter is planting his pine,
I hear Des, in his speckled gansey and green beret,
ordering whiskey-and-pep, demanding
'What'll you have, Pearse?' exhorting 'That'll
settle your stummick,' when we clink glasses tá
'an iolar i mbárr na píne,
's an traona sa neanntóig,' Cervantes and Sancho
are riding Clavileño, the wooden Pegaso,
Symons calling Ibsen 'a giant who can fly',
and Unamuno is mocking,
                              single-handed,
the mockers last of all.

Whenever I smell a rose I hear
a trandafír breathing.
When I clutch you, Abelard would envy me,
and I would envy Cavafy,
the new broad spear Shaka invented
goes down before the guns,
the claymore crumbles at Culloden,
the furze doors part,
a Chinese poet, parting, says:
dasz einer des andern Freund sei,
and I remember a friend's cool, brave, loving kiss
in a crowded bar off the Haymarket,
and the beautiful, sudden, brief coolness of his body
when he came back, one morning, to the warm bed.

The past is alive in us now,
near to its high native rock.

The black and white of this world

Kuruntokai praises a flower:
   petals white, stem black —
women wear it in their hair.

   We need that flower,
and we need another:
   petals black, stem white:
for men to wear in their hair.

A black-petalled,
   white-stemmed flower
for women's hair.

   A white-petalled
black-stemmed flower
   for men to wear.

Bright after Dark

for Sebastian Ryan

In the first country,
what you must do when the cow stops giving milk
is climb, after dark, a certain hill,
and play the flute: to kill your scheming neighbour's curse.
If you can find a silver flute to play,
the spell will break all the faster, the surer.
But silver is not essential. But: the job must
be done after dark:
otherwise, it won't work.

In the second country,
when you send a child out of the house at night,
after dark, you must, if you wish it well,
take, from the fire, a burnt-out cinder
and place it on the palm of the child's hand
to guard the child against the dangers of the dark.
The cinder, in this good function, is called aingeal,
meaning angel.

In the third country,
if you take a journey at night, above all
in the blind night of ebony, so good for witches to work in,
you dare not rely on fireflies for light,
for theirs is a brief, inconstant glow. What you must hope
is that someone before you has dropped grains of maize
on the ground to light your way; and you must drop
grains of maize for whoever comes after you:
for only maize can light the way on a dark night.

Lovers

You with full hands
keep them closed, like fists;
use the warm wealth you clutch in there
only for loading blows;
a hundred birds in a cage on the latch:
none of the birds can fly.
But at times you forget, relax,
the knuckles unwhiten,
a grain of warmth slips out between fingers.
Feathers move gently.

While I advance vainly, blowing my top,
professionally proffering my open
wide wide open palms,
for all comers to lick.
Splayed. Eager. Empty.
Not even a tearlet of sweat.
Would-be generous, poor.

It still happens

Try to forgive this: I once found you gentle —
believing that the greatest thing to be —
and told you so: a strong hand thwacked the counter:
'I want more to be violent!' Oh you were gaily drunk;
but have achieved, soberly, that gay wish.

Now my excess demand for gentleness
and your impatience drive us both to violence
only unearthly gentleness might cure;
the courtesy that, once a week, for a second,
we grant each other, may seem frail to critics.

But wears the years down well: it still happens.

Jasmine or Basalt or Bread

Where even carnations were kept —
except by those licensed half-shockers
    the college-boys —
for weddings, like furtive bonfires
on fading st. john's night fiestas,
    I grew my youth.

Where no one might sport dandelion:
bright yellow, perhaps — but a weed;
    and having learnt,
good prig, that shit-lesson too early,
I adored wild valerian on walls
    but left my coat grey.

Where later discovering cider
and almost a mind of my own
    I wore nine times
bright weeds like a bride not a widow
till rebels more cautioned by cost
    made me conform.

Where more truth, they claimed, could be lost
by obvious quirks of defiance
    than cunning gained —
though I wanted not protest but colour
to sing in my coat at the sun
    or give to a hand.

Now walking between the valerians,
my hand twisting stems I don't dare
    wear in my coat,
too frightened of phantoms and facts,
I wish to make clear, in mid-forties'
    dour alloyed voice:

Where the young may not wear dandelions
or ear-rings or beards in their joy
    at discovering the world
is small room for old men or rose-trees,
for basalt or jasmine or bread:
    but only for death.

Inter-Crevice Memo

The rest of the tribe may be slower than you
at reading your symptoms, the small and the true:
how, taking an interest, you find that obsession
a year or two later has taken possession;
and a meaningless, unbreakable habit grows
from the careful, occasional, defiant pose.

The rest may be slower to recognize both
a new decay and a fresh growth;
but when you've named and filed nine,
the pack may be scenting the fifth sign.

Though much that you fancy as pure give-away
does not exist any more than Cathay,
no matter how beige or goodwilled their intentions
they too are given to rich and wild inventions.

Near Adrigole

A sow's eleven teats
just like the teeth of a rake.

Lean cows on sandy grass:
backbones like boats upturned.

Syde

for Peter Mew

Stone placed out for the frost to split
into roof-tile sizes; every limestone house-top softer with —
not like slate — green moss,
lichen white or yellow.

One man still, in Duntisbourne Lear,
who knows that old skill, like a thatcher.
Slate victorious everywhere else,
easier, unfrutiful, no moss or lichen
for the sun to alight on.

But the warm drystone walls
remember Carna, Chavín, grow Visigothic;
neat narrow layers like slate itself
at Cadaqués, at Corofin —
south-facing walls grow whiter lichen,
glowed here and there with yellow,
north-facing walls blotch damper green with moss,
white confronting green
across a narrow lane,
South confronting North
across a field too small to last much longer
the wheat's invasion of a sheep realm,
the tractors greeding ample spaces breaking
the walls, the wild life, green wolds browning
Sussex-maroon, Castilian gold.

Jurassic gravel: warm colour —
petit-beurre, Limburg cheese,
double Gloucester? fawn, cinnamon,
light-brown sugar, tawny Málaga foothills:
this gravel retains, reveals, plant-shapes, birds —
yellow bittern? cicada?

Not bittern: that gravel's grey-blue, cold.
Let's go to Glencree to get warm.
Cicada's a tremble of light on the face
of Ciren church and down the street we'll buy
warm-as-gravel-coloured homemade fudge.
Enormous chunks,
brown-sugar mouth.

Boxing the Fox

We rode the canals
   we steered the locks
we may have caught scabies
   but never the pox
we were happy just cruising
   and boxing the fox
cruising the rivers of Dublin and
   foxing the cops
               some of the *time*
               some of the time
cruising the rivers and
   boxing the fox

Across the orchards of custom,
   over the high wall of law,
over hatred's broken glass,
   past fear's envious claw,
we reached our own true rivers,
   the rivers of your hair,
and peace as brief as man's contempt
   came through and healed us there.
And who's to know but some small stream
   from the rivers of your care
may break their broken glass
   and be their cure and care.

We rode the canals
   we steered the locks
we may have caught scabies
   but never the pox
we were happy just cruising
   and boxing the fox
cruising the rivers of Dublin and
   foxing the cops
               some of the *time*
               some of the time

cruising the rivers and
    boxing the fox

We dodged around begrudgers,
    stuck in many a weary craw,
for snobs and hypocrites became
    the antepenultimate straw.
But we boxed the fox of jealousy,
    and slept in the glens of your hair,
and pleasure as long as man's contempt
    came down and kept us there.
And who's to know but a lucky drop
    from the beauty of your sweat
could melt their batons of hatred,
    and be their saviour yet.

We rode the canals
    we steered the locks
we may have caught scabies
    but never the pox
we were happy just cruising
    and boxing the fox
cruising the rivers of Dublin and
    foxing the cops
                    some of the *time*
                    some of the time
cruising the rivers and
    boxing the fox

Wrinkled Knuckles

Burns' Nicht

to the air of 'Fuígfidh mise an baile seo'

We never made Glencullen
but we drank in Blessington opposite the arch
and in the Old Bawn we sang
Bonnie Charlie and Carrickfergus and the long black veil
(and in Kilkenny it is reported
there are marble stones there as black as ink).
And we toasted Pòl Crùbach and other brave makars
though who's to reckon what flasks they'd break
to our later diversions —
but we have eyes
as warm as theirs
and what we want is
not greatly different.

It's even conceivable they might contract
a social disease.

And one day we took a bus to the Zoo
but stopped for a drink in the last pub,
and never made the beasts;
but you told me stories of your life
and sang a song in Finnish,
we clinked glasses: 'Kiipis' —
and we did make Ryan's of Parkgate Street:
glowing wood, shining brass —

With songs and stories and a kiss or two,
it's not the leaving of Liverpool that grieves me

All the Old Gems

1

Once you looked
                far
                    into my eyes.

Our unbearable ignorance:
our indispensable ignorance.

Once we looked far
into one another's eyes,
gaze travelling down gaze
like tongues down mouths
in a deep kiss
as though down the very throat
right to the heart, the gizzard;
eyes travelling down eyes
as though right to the soul.

Our unbearable ignorance:
our indispensable ignorance.

Yet a few times we've entered
a fleeting knowledge of each other,
illusive or true;
a knowledge like pennies
filched from dead eyelids,
or sudden bountiful windfalls
(never mind a bruise or two).

Our unbearable
indispensable

2

I sit in the deep armchair watching
your naked sleeping,
diagonal across the narrow bed,
your legs well apart, your lips
only a little; but for your eyes
and the fingers of one hand
behind your head,
not an inch of you is hidden:
my gaze can travel, graze,
all that slender grace.
But I've no call to touch you now,
to look is enough
and is calm.
Never, my dear,
a more beautiful body.
So from morning till noon I sit here
watching, and reading, and waiting.

3

Sometimes I lift the dark
dark brown, almost black
hair to kiss your nape
and before I can eat
I'm stopped in my tracks
I can never believe my eyes:
it looks so young *so*
young. I thought *you* were young
but it looks years younger still
and so white
and so smooth
and so soft
so I kiss
so I kiss.

It's fucking well heartbreaking
so it is it's heart-fucking-breaking
and is a glory of God
and makes the heart whole.

    4

corduroy dancer
corpo delgado
at a basement party
at 2 in the morning
pastora imperio
and paddy moloney
are playing for you
and the bossa nova

in light-brown regalia
that takes to your body
as close as a lover
you're like — to my frenzy —
a banderillero
but never quite murderous
flamenco dancer
but mostly more gentle

so what can *I* do
but shrug out the colours
and lust and wait

or now with macdara
playing bar-billiards
at 6 in the evening
gloved in this corduroy
suit of brown lights
your movements are dances

though music is silent —
how I envy that table

but what can be done
only worship and watch
and lust and wait

flask
     wand

5

One morning your hand raw-looking and swollen; sore.
You'd banged it, fisted, over and over, against walls and railings
the night before in wild dismay: my greed had betrayed you,
my lunacy driven you: 'always the soft idiot, softly: me'.

We sat beside each other gazing at your hand. I wanted to
die, but I couldn't speak; afraid of apology insulting.

'I've got wrinkled knuckles,' you said, cheering up a little.
As once before I felt the splendour — even the terror — of
your power to forgive. So we started trotting out all the old
gems.

It reminded me, though, for the first time in years, what it
was like to slam a drunken hand against the walls and railings,
hitting one's heart, the other's heart, perhaps weeping,
stumbling home late.

When you leave this town, I may commit once more that
rite of anguish. But may the road rise with you, homeward,
blessing can survive the rite of pain: which won't last more
than a night or two, for I'll have your gifts to learn, your
lessons to enjoy.

I pray to your gods and mine — we share some — to
guard you always from the wild rites of the swollen hand,
from those who'd harm you into them. Or else to drive you
deep into their arms.

And when you've gone I'll kiss my knuckles towards your

country, and with any luck all the old gems will come dazzling and somersaulting and ricochetting through the skies from your town to mine, from my town to yours, and once in a blue sun we'll send them back to each other wrapped up in greetings. Thole. Celebrations.

In the morning
Flowering knuckles
When you rise

Copper-beech and butter-fingers

'en ti como sol' — Octavio Paz

You made me feel so young again
that imagining I was over eighty,
basking in a second
but more precocious childhood,
I started climbing trees
to bring you down the moon growing
on every tree-top.

But always a branch broke,
or my butter-fingers lost their hold,
and I fell to the ground
(never mind the bruises),
clutching perhaps a torn leaf —
copper-beech or baobab —
as a peace-offering or ersatz.

So instead of me fetching you the moon
I turn to you to give me back again
the sun: en ti como sol.

But I mustn't feel such
a failure after all:
in certain lights the copper-beech-leaf
looks almost the same colour as your hair
and eyes,
       blends
            into your rioting hair.

But I mustn't feel too cocky after all:
no leaf compares to your body's
whitegold slender grace:
on whom how soon
must these butter-fingers lose their
adoring gluttonous contrite grateful
so precarious but miraculous foothold?

To bring Posada back from the grave; or,
   Let me be the skeleton in your cupboard

When 44
         falls in love
                     with 21
When a desert
            falls in love
                        with a jungle-stream
When a ruined gizzard
                  falls in love
                              with a quenchless thirst
When a skeleton
              falls in love
                          with a corduroy dancer
When jealousy
            falls in love
                        with freedom

When la Belle et la Bête mate
it's enough to bring Posada back from the grave:
Listen well: already you can hear his skeleton
spider-jiving, scrabbling for his burin.
Let's hope, for his sake, they built the coffin
of box-wood, let's hope, for my sake, they forgot
to pack the muslin —
                     To cut the mustard
I've still a yearning, so:

Let me be the skeleton in your cupboard:
I swear I'd never try to get out:
I'd be golden browning up the deathwatch-beetle
and carving my doggerel, your name,
gently on the inside walls. Your name,
your name on the dark walls.

Clearing

Not mine but yours
not mine but your own

My ram-riding fire-fish
my dark dawn
my pine-grove in the sun
on a headland over a bay
my early morning summer sun
my clearing in the jungle
my swan
        lion
            tangle
my mouth-music
my scream
my rumplefyke

My tiny golden bull
just out of the toril
poised

My nights in the gardens of Asturias
my black joker my singer
my poet in New York

My Turku
my Akureyri
my Newfoundland

My humming-bird my burning bush
my red earth my black olives
my sloe
        bracken
                almond-oil
my glowing aqueduct
over a dry river-bed

my bright brown stream
in a Wicklow forest
my dear dark head

Not mine but yours
not mine but your own

My friend

Clearing

Fountains Ankle-High

for Francesc Parcerisas

Black wine in Bràfim
Green wine in Queluz
Across the yearning desert
sundering March and Martim
colour becomes a heart:
the heart keeps colour

Green wine in Bragança
Black wine in Sueca
Till all the seas gang dry,
my love, the Tagus flows
into the Latin brine

Anselm, that Muslim saint
of Compostela, listen:
in a slender dancer
before a Vigo altar
God with his lover blent

Thick black wine
Slender green
Like Andalusian-Arab
ankle-fountains calling
across the rock may yet
redeem the monolith

December '73

Eight Lines

'Who d'you think you're kidding?'
　'We're easy to mistake:
fear can look forbidding,
　lust can look like hate.'

'Who d'you think you're kidding?'
　'Not even our own mistake:
loneliness for bedding,
　death for a mate.'

Sauvetage

The small thin fish like caraway seed
in the mad cake of the slip-water shallow,
the oars bright-yellow
with bright-red blades in the yellow boat:
'sauvetage'. Beyond, the river itself,
the deep water a deep green,
betrayed into blue by distance only
and the lake
that under the mountain's challenge
cannot abandon convention.

The small thin fish like caraway seed
sewn so loose in the shifting shallow,
a mim shadow
for every skinny seed-fish.
Thin, not slim, and scarcely 'golden-brown',
drest in bright colours, a boy
invades the bright boat, and lies,
face down,
at length in it; and with his barbarous hands
the boat rocks, the slip-water, and the slim black fish.

Accustomed to set my cap
at flamenco, gazelle, the baroque, the perfect,
I am betrayed (mildly)
by a nakedness of legs, thin-ness
unmasking grace, and the deep-blue alpargatas
close together — slightly absurd things
for at least once, to one lack, attractive.
And so renounce desire
and the menace of the boat marked 'sauvetage'.

Knife-Day

for Alan

A man looked up at the blue-and-white sky to say,
below his breath but fiercely:
'If You live, don't let her die
under the knife — whatever you are,
her, or him, or it.'
Then brainwashed-guilty, lowered his head
to glare down
at window-sill, shed, overgrown garden,
withering bicycle — 'if that's where you are' —
down, down, swivelled his glare to where
an hour ago he'd poured chloride of lime
into the corpse of a dustbin alive
with millions — 'Maybe that's where you are,
in one or all of those struggling white worms
struggling in summer joy or against death,
or now still';
but though he clutched the pink wooden
chest-of-drawers top and leaned forward
till his chest met the rim of the tallish
tumbler, his tie got froth,
his nose nearly touched the pane, he couldn't
see the metal carrion on the landing
of the back-door steps, but only
plastic pastel clothes-pegs on a line,
so he'd used up, for now, his abusive imagination,
and couldn't imagine God
as or in
a peg. So he just looked straight ahead
into the summer trees,
at ten or twelve wild roses
in the foreground overgrowing garden,
and said: 'Let her go on living.
She deserves to live at least as well as You
deserve to live. She deserves death less.'

Monastic Luxury

The cult Paresse
has mainly doubting priests. One monk, this morning,
   not heeding Brother Pérez's purist warning,
went up and washed his hair;
                      and where
magnificence of evening weight had been
   resilience, not puffball but spring, was seen.
Racing incredulous, wide-open hands
   through this new hint of lithe heretical lands,
he walked around the garden and the house,
   the dusty chapel and the cluttered cells,
feeling re-born — as if an old souse
   could, after one dry day, become
a child again, with a toy drum,
   his first communion sins, and caramels.
The monk rushed up to ring the rusty bells,
   tugging the sweat-free rope. What cleanliness foretells —
a head of hair like sunlight inside sun,
   remission for the weak, peace to the strong —
he would announce to the baldest nun,
   the blindest lizard, the most mocking song.
His hair, at any moment, he knew, would flame,
   would fly away, bearing him into fame,
but he'd be shining, cleansed. He'd change his name,
   his nation, and his habits . . . All as though
to feel curious, an odd time, were to know.

In real though ignominious distress,
   a slightly-younger-slightly-older one
went up to wash his face;
                 in place
of glass his mirror was goatskin trimmed with lace.
   For some time after he'd begun
the lathering he went on thinking of
   some aspects of what he mistook for love;
and so instead of crests and ripples
   caused a tumult of suds and bubbles;

and one of those fine globes of air and light
    was of such time and girth, splendour and height,
he got to know it, let it seem to choose
    its own moment of boredom; then, gone wild
(small boy again — as though a fulltime child
    outside the walls would share her secret news),
he played a while, rubbing and bursting and sloshing;
    but finally, on getting down to washing,
one of the bright globes broke on his red brow,
    and for a sudden private singing second
life was all imperious youth had reckoned,
    he was clean like a star, the book of kings was now.
As he walked cellward, studying how not to tell
    this nonsense out, a meaningless cracked bell
came barely to his ears. All his thoughts had run
    as weak or strong as water back to water, air, and light.
As though a childish choice can be undone
    by children's fancy . . . As if one
good metaphor half-chanced on a winter's day
    could always keep oblivion away.

Movement

The blind men stumble round
a small, unmoving bird
they feel is brightly coloured
on a grey field.

A True Story of Art and Friendship

When Paul Funge came to my house for the painting he brought in the station-wagon not only the obvious materials — and an easel — but a bottle of sherry and a bottle of Aurum, a pound of the best kidneys to be extortioned for in Rathmines, a flamenco guitar and a repertoire to match it.

He stood at the easel with his back to the window, I sat in the deep armchair begetter of endless years of unforgivable sloth, we both had glasses within easy reach of the hand. Now and again we talked.

When the painting was done the painter sang and played: 'Mi marido es un minero', the Dies Irae, Whack-fol-the-diddle and many more. When the singing was done the guitarist went into the kitchen and cooked riñones al jerez, the best I've ever eaten. When the meal was over the chef began to sing again but after a while the drink ran out so we had to face the pub.

Never was a portrait so happily painted.

European Prayer

Cabral: Cabral:
we beg forgiveness but
beg even more for help.

Cabral: can you hear us?
We're scrabbling, desperate,
earth in our broken beaks:
we let them murder you:
don't let them murder us.

No, wait. Your silence means
you must be angry, we
put that badly, listen:

For Christ's sake have pity.
Use your influence. Sanctions —
no (take Christ back), for? for
— we never troubled to learn
the name of your —
your people's god, or gods;
we let our christ crusade,
we burnt him at the stake
of our crusades, we take
back now, in panic,
those godlings we called saints.

Your invaders, our loving lairds,
for trusting centuries
did us the dirt at home.

    (The coffin-ships you died in
    built some beautiful buildings)

But no: the old arrogance nudges
even this abject need.
And we *are* abject now:

You were not one of the haters.
You never hated us because
our skin is white
(whiskey-purple / grime-grey).

Even your sacred places, fouled
by our incurable pride,
could not make you hate us —
would not let you hate us:
that's why men killed you,
and though we let them kill you,
the secret of such love,
beyond our scope, must grow
still greater against death:

so it's you, you only,
we beg. Beg. Demand! —
Cabral, can you hear us?
Can you hear *me*?

Senhor d'ajuda!
Ora pro nobis.

> Bekizwe and Cabral,
> somewhere in the darkness,
> dark as European hearts,
> white as death,
> wished for the power
> to love again.

Lament

Lament has no real vocative:
in the name of mercy
a merciless lie.

There isn't anywhere Bekizwe
   meets Cabral
There is no place for me to stuff potatoes
   down Cobbett's gullet
or clearances for him and me persuade
   'the sheep are as beautiful'

Nowhere Cabral and Bekizwe
   convert Swart

Starlings and sheep-bells
Starlings and sheep-bells but no place
   for Edward the Second and Lorca
to compare notes
   No room in the caves of Clashmealcon
no room on the pure heights
                  of Ricurishca

There is no place where living death
can tell the dead: We loved you
   there is no room for amends
There isn't anywhere
                sloth can praise
There was never a place the people
of Casas Viejas were told
             how Chile mourned
Nor anywhere posterity can tell us:
Those people you killed in our name
   are dancing with us now to thank you
there isn't anywhere the Chilean dead
hear of mourning or millenniums

Mercy: stateless as ever
Nansen: light-years dead

Sometimes lament is a plural society,
sometimes a singular lie.

Okigbo graces no court-room
You and me,
                    Luis with Carles,
may break but nowhere bless the bread
mercy pretends we sowed

Slave-Chains

for Francis Devine

How many slaves ever begged the conqueror:
   make me less human —
though many after a time can learn to ask:
   make me less than human
and in the end oppressor and oppressed
   may come to screeching at each other
     dumbly beseeching one another:
   make me less human —
     scatophagous collaborators
rebel and hireling swap their quisling roles
   gunman and gunfodder swapping
trying to reach and breach one another
   retching at last the answer
     to this mad maiden's prayer:
   my chains of evil office
     are far too light:
       enslave me deeper still.

How many slaves or freemen ever begged:
   come and oppress me —
though might may beg the bodies it kneels on:
   make me less

Mozarabic Wine

Drinking Mozarabic wine
we played Buraku music
in the gardens beyond the porchless ghettoes,
in the gardens planted by black slaves,
each one the price of a garden.
The harpsichords fountained fireworks.

Drinking Mozarabic music
till it fountained out of our eardrums,
we sang the wine but never
let them listen in the slums:
'they'd only drink it.'

We were too holy to plant a vine ourselves,
we let the blacks and phony Christians delve
but with growing eagerness
drank their green music.
We were far too proud and clean
to carve and hollow and string,
but once the wood was polished and vibrant
we played the instruments and called them ours.

If a slave with a blue birthmark dared
to play the glinting vibrant wood he'd shaped for us,
we ordered other slaves to cut his hands off,
keeping our clean hands clean.

If a gardener drank the fruit of his toiling music,
the poet-princes tholed, could even praise him,
but later our stricter cousins
rammed the glass in his face,
and never guessed the colour of his blood.

If a slave played,
if a gardener drank,

our clean hands were seldom too atrophied for justice
(what's a slave or two, a gardener or twenty?
the labour-fountain dances to the tune).

We owned ourselves musicians but seldom drunkards.
We owned musicians — preferably blind —
and thought we owned ourselves.
We never heard the music they kept playing
with fishfingers in their porchless ghettoes
on instruments not made for our dreams, kept from our wits.
Our flowering trees and amorous rivulets deafened us.

So when the slaves and gardeners
erupted out of their slums,
with a crude poet or two just less afraid of them than of us
    and our couplets,
they burned the music and spurned the poets with wine,
mistaking crudeness for elegance —
so crudely had our true elegance
burned their hungry stumps, their forebears' pride.
In the sober silence we forced them to make,
we cannot even atone.

According to Bigotry

'I was born with a blue birthmark
under my left armpit.'

  'I was born with a blood-stained
  right hand stuck to my head.'

  'After the battle they found
  most of our dead had tails.'

Driscoll in Dublin

for Gerard Kamanga,
because he liked it

Someone who thought he might some day be a great poet (otherwise: 'hopes to write one good line before he dies') was sitting drinking in a Dublin pub with three companions, each of whom cherished the same suspicion about himself.

An African man came in, with an African woman. They sat on stools at the bar. In a row on their bench against the wall the four great poets gazed at the newcomers with variegated interest.

That's the first time I ever saw any niggers in this pub, said one great poet, caressing a source-book with the ball of his thumb.

Must it be 'niggers'? Driscoll asked.

Why not?

Because they might not like hearing it.

Why not?

Attempting, 'as' in a nightmare, to explain, Driscoll lost his temper. Anger is all the worse when you have to whisper it.

You know, Drisc, the second poet said, about the colour question you're pathological.

You are indeed, said the first great poet.

Indeed you are, said the third great poet.

Driscoll went off in the lowest of dudgeons.

Five days later someone who really was a great poet, and had written several great poems all about love, craned across the quiet bar towards Driscoll at its other end, and called loudly to him: You love niggers, don't you?

Driscoll Rides Again

White humour.
A white comedy.
A white day for Africa.
As white as pitch.
Only whites and Irish need apply.
Kenya's white-hearted
black mountains —

Driscoll went round, stumbling, blinded by blackwash,
whiteballed; imagining a life where white might be sportive
that often.

The Slaves Come Back to Haunt Him
   as He Reads

'Armchair hyena:
our suffering your food.'

'Birds can eat the berries off the yew-tree:
they sluice the tiny poisonous core
harmless through their monstrous bodies,
nourished on what, if humans ate, would kill.
So I devour your martyrdom,
to slouch off (I call it flying)
and belch into even louder song
about my suffering brothers — '

'When humans like us would have died:
when humans, like us, died.

Armchair hyena:
our death your feast.'

Flyting

GOD   Would you give your life to rid humanity of
racialism?

DRISCOLL   Perhaps. Dead-drunk? Incontinent at 90, or
fearing cancer.

GOD   You mean No.

DRISCOLL   Yes.

GOD   Would you put your hand in the fire for it?

DRISCOLL   No.

GOD   Would you work down the mines for it?

DRISCOLL   No.

GOD   Then stick to that fairy-wand.

Achnasheen

for Eoghan Ó Néill

'You'd miss the Gaelic from the placenames,'
you said, turning from the danger-seat to me in the back
      swigging Talisker,
driving through Wester Ross making for the Kyle of
      Lochalsh.
And the next signpost we came to was Achnasheen.

How could there be any Gaelic 'for' Achnasheen?
It isn't Gaelic any more. It could never be English.
Despite the murderous maps,
despite the bereft roadsigns,
despite the casual distortions of illiterate scribes,
the name remains beautiful. A maimed beauty.

Hiding behind it somewhere
its real name.

You'd almost think the conquerors thought
Gaelic was God:
its real name unnameable.

And I remembered the first-time crossing the Border,
not the Highland Line but the one from Cavan into
      'Ulster',
and missing the Gaelic placenames, the maiming ugliness of
      that;
guessing the real names, failing to guess, the irk of that,
like a horsehair down the back.

The Gaelic names beating their wings madly
behind the mad cage of English;
the new names half the time transparent, but half the time
silent as the grave
                  English would bury Irish in.

Later we saw Beinn Ailleagan: the jewelled mountain —
but not called that but keeping its true name:
Beinn Ailleagan
                        wearing its name like a jewel
upon its snow-white breast
                                    like the jewel of the Gaelic tongue
that old men and young women keep shining and singing
all over the Catholic islands and the Calvinist
islands for all the invader
and his canting quisling ministers could reek.

And will the black sticks of the devil, Eoghan,
ever pipe us into heaven at last —
as one night down the torchlit street of Áth Dara —
into a heaven of freedom to give
things back
                    their true names?

Like streets in Barcelona,
like Achnasheen,
Belfast

The Frost is All Over

for Michael Hartnett

To kill a language is to kill a people.
The Aztecs knew far better: they took over
their victims' language, kept them carving
obsidian beauties, weeded their religion
of dangerous gentleness, and winged them blood-flowers
(that's a different way to kill a people).
The Normans brought and grew, but Honor Croome
could never make her Kerryman verse English:
Traherne was in the music of his tears.

We have no glint or caution who we are:
our patriots dream wolfhounds in their portraits,
our vendors pose in hunting-garb, the nightmare
forelock tugging madly at some lost leash.
The Vikings never hurt us, xenophilia
means bland servility, we insult
ourselves and Europe with artificial trees,
and coins as gelt of beauty now
as, from the start, of power.

Like Flemish words on horseback, tongue survives
in turns of speech the telly must correct;
our music bows and scrapes on the world's platforms,
each cat-gut wears a rigorous bow-tie.
The frost, we tell them, is all over, and they love
our brogue so much they give us guns to kill
ourselves, our language, and all the other gooks.

Bobrowski would have understood, he found
some old, surviving words of a murdered language,
and told a few friends; but he knew how to mourn,
a rare talent, a need not many grant.

To call a language dead before it dies
means to bury it alive; some tongues do die

from hours or days inside the coffin, and when
the tearful killers dig it up they find
the tongue, like Suarez, bitten to its own bone.
Others explode in the church, and stain the bishop,
whose priest could speak no Gaelic to his 'flock'
but knew to sink a splendid tawny goblet
as deep as any master of the hunt.

Is Carleton where the tenderness must hide?
Or would they have the Gaelic words, like insects,
crawl up the legs of horses, and each bite,
or startle, be proclaimed a heritage?
Are those who rule us, like their eager voters,
ghosts yearning for flesh? Ghosts are cruel,
and ghosts of suicides more cruel still.
To kill a language is to kill one's self.

Summer 1973

Pibroch

for Robert Somerset

Boarding the coffin-ship for Canada,
paying their pittance to the foreign owners,
the clansmen found their piper lacked even that.
They could not face the far sea without music,
for the new land, that strange planet,
they needed the music of their own lost land.

So they begged the masters to let the piper
play his passage. But the masters of money
turned the pauper away,
money as always having no mercy on music,
except the music of its own blind, gaping wound.

So the people in their need scraped around in their poverty
and mustered the pittance for the music to travel,
and so the masters made a little more money,
but the festering hold was dancing,
lamentation swabbed the landless deck,
the creaking, rotting boat was outraged and blest.

Cat Rua

The light-red kitten flexing its forearms in the grass.

Under the slide by the wall to the left of the back garden. Opposite, under the right-hand slide, one magpie.

In the mild morning light, neither bright nor dim, the young cat stretches out its left forepaw to full stretch; at this distance — peering from behind curtains — I can't really tell whether its claws are at full stretch or not; but I'd imagine so.

The cat's arm looks rigid, determined; its colour, the colour of the whole body, is incredibly beautiful to look at — what used to be called 'tortoiseshell', only a fair bit lighter.

Bird and cat are frozen in their attitudes, for one of those moments that seems much longer than a clock or a human could measure or diminish.

The magpie, every bit as beautiful in its blue and black and white as the cat, no matter what its morals may be, stands obviously bristling: frozen in proud courage.

The kitten keeps stretching its arm, then slightly bends it; but doesn't retract.

Then from the pear-tree above the right-hand slide, above the brave magpie, another magpie alights; not exactly shoulder to shoulder, but near enough.

For another immeasurable second, cat and birds gaze at each other; measure.

Then the first magpie rises ever so slightly off the ground, flaps its wings, and subsides — and before it's touched the ground again the kitten, God help it (no doubt scared out of its wits), is streaking faster than a blue flame back to the human safety of the house.

I never saw a cat move so fast.

The Cap

The cap I wanted to wear tonight I couldn't lay hands on:
light-brown crumpled corduroy
forgotten overnight in a flat I was two years transient in
by a Ballyconnell truck-driver. When Francis came round
    the next morning
he said 'It's raining, you lost your best beret last week and can't
    find one in the whole of Leeds:
keep the cap. Peter makes good money, loses a cap a month,
    buys a new cap every month.'
Peter I'd never try to imitate
the way you put the hint of a liquid *y*
between the *c* and the *a* in that word cap.
But Peter it kept my head warm and dry
for two long years and more. I brought it across on the plane,
had to cram it on because of the driving tarmac rain,
it made a couple of customs-officers look crooked at me.
I had my hands deep
in the pockets of a plastic mac
and that was sopping too,
but Peter the main road to Cavan gets kinder every ell,
warmer every magpie, every barefoot blackbird.

Brown with No Whites

for Michael Augustin

A young brown pony in a green Gloucester field
trotting gently up to a mottled wall
dandling its big head across looking for company.

Giant brown eyes, unanswerable, softly questing,
no whites.
           A timid human hand was not repulsed.

From our side a dove-grey pregnant cat
climbed in a stately fashion across the wall
to bask in sunlight on a stone slab
                 near the pony,

Who warily bent the sturdy neck down
to nuzzle the microscopic furry creature —
fellow, perhaps, creature —
and friends were made. She rolled around on the warm
   grey stone,
the pony moved her about with his nose, they played tip-
   and-tig and conkers, they played like lovers
who never guessed that love could be anything but fun.
The pony and the cat making friends made a human being
   happy.

But then someone told him, in friendly jest,
the name of the pony was
Leprechaun.
           (As who might say Shillelagh, Rastus, Brit.)
Green English fields turned orange —
like a decoration on a Cabinet-Minister's breast;
the wall grew higher between the pony and me.

But no pony deserves a name so tawdry;
so the same human hand, less timid now,

reached out again and, even less repulsed,
re-named this animal — what's in a pony's name? —
a name less flippant, a friend's name,
a tree's name.
Other trees bore witness to that rechristening:
apple, sycamore, holly.
Gloucester fields turned green again,
the sky as blue again
                         as ever over Wormwood Scrubs.
'Macdara', said the man to the pony,
'play with your heavy grey cat. A mhac', ar sé,
'ná bí ag briseadh cait: brisfear luath go leor í.'
Wishing human beings had never called each other names
less than human, less than ponies, less than cats.
The cat went on playing with the pony,
like plover basking in a meadow full of sheep.

She Made her False Name Real

When the Holy Office descended upon us to make us all
   saints,
to change our names with tongues of flame,
to make us all saints instead of the devils they
knew
      we
        were
              under pain of all those tongues,
of turning not living devils but most unholy ghosts,
we changed our names, not being martyrs, to the names
   they gave us.

A change of name's a trivial thing:
it only leads to centuries of bitterness.

Nahara ben Abrafim became
                     Arnau Albertí
and remained a good Catholic for ever.
Isach Leví became
           Bernat Aguiló.
Mahabuf Faquim became
           Joan Amat —
he was John the Beloved for ever.
Magaluf ben Salem became
               Pere Cases.

What Marc Despont was called before the change
nobody knows:
              his Jewish name is not recorded.
What Joan Martí was called before the change
is not recorded:
              perhaps a descendant of his,
changing only one vowel,
gave his life for the freedom of Cuba.

Jacob Prehensal became
Andreu Rossinyol: Andrew the Nightingale.
Felip Umbert had been
                    Isach ben Magaluf.

When every convert on the island sported
   a brand-new holy name,
the priests came round to smoke out infidel vestiges.
We all hastened to bless ourselves and bless ourselves and
   bless ourselves, not being martyrs,
only carpenters and tailors and bookbinders
and the best cartographers in Europe,
yes we all blessed ourselves like crazy
except an old woman called Jaumeta
whose surname is not recorded
nor even her first name before the change.
But she was imprisoned for eight days on bread-and-
      water —
mild enough for our enlightened times —
and that old woman made her name real,
she made the name the Christians forced upon her
Jewish and real and Christian beyond their burning.

The Flames are False: Only the Hell is Real

for Carmelo Sánchez

My name was Gaietà Ripoll, if I had lived
in your enlightened times I'd have had to sign
myself not Gaietà
but Cayetano, like,
as in this limbo some drowned men enlighten me,
Dudley for Darach.

Not only my name they distorted:
progress distorted their vengeance:
for I had the privilege of being the last
culprit the Holy Office killed.
They should have burnt me,
but they only hanged me:
the Church, like mankind, was making headway.
Shamefaced, they were *shame*-faced.
But nostalgic.

So shame and nostalgia, as creative a mésalliance
as Christ and the moneychangers, painted a cardboard
    expanse
with flames, the flames of hell, the glory-holes of their own
    minds,
the purgatories of their misnomers;
that cardboard hellfire held beneath my gallows,
until my dancing stopped.
I danced above their cardboard flames.
Their compromise between shame and bloodlust
drizzled
            above the phoney flames of bad faith.
My name was Gaietà Ripoll. My last words were:
Crec en Déu.

The Kid on the Mountain

for Vincent Woods

What colours can we call them,
the earth and stone that took our eyes in youth,
and now come back with all the pain and beauty
of lost youth itself?

Light-brown,
                    fawn,
umber, sienna, inaccuracies,
even honey: that old myth.

The colour, the shade,
                              changes
from stone to stone in the same building,
from field to foothill.

Warmth
not heat:
warmth built by human hands for the heat to warm,
and for the centuries of eyes, our eyes,
to warm their hands at,
to warm our speaking hearts at.

Warmth by light out of time:
a mane of colour streaming down
the soft hard back of time.

When I was twenty-seven the Málaga foothills
the light-brown colour of a young goat caught
on Kilmashogue when I was eleven then skittering out of
    our grasp
then caught again, kept; the nap, the burlap eye-feeling,
of clay and kid.

Climbing the light — never say pale, never —
brown foothills on the opposite slope
across the dry river the goats were black

but kept in the mind as a rough, soft, warm fawn
was kept on Kilmashogue for a day, let go,
but kept in the mind until its river dries.

Climbing we heard and saw
cicadas 'a tremble of light in the leaves' of the olive-trees
and rapping the trees' rough skin, hurting knuckles,
we put their tremble out
                                for a long minute but then
they started up again:
they were the sound of heat and the earth was the colour
    of warmth.

Remember at thirty-four (was that still beauty and pain?)
crossing the Pyrenean frontier breaking bread together,
for the first time together in that beloved country,
the good strong Spanish bread that needs no butter —
the countryside a disappointing green:
that wasn't what we came for, that wasn't our need
(but theirs, but theirs!)
the fierce red earth
in the olive-orchards — that was a different nettle,
we grasped it with all our eyes and how it stung us
into life and how we stung it back!

But the calm
            light
                    brown
the golden stone
the myth of honey serene on golden churches
the shades
            changing
from brick to brick from Font

Romeu to Sant Climent:
serene stone
answering a sky that's both serene and fierce
the silent stone speaking in colour
one colour answering another
one silence speaking
to the other: Hands
climbing the sky through fashioned earth,
bringing the earth and sky together,
stone breathing time,
a compact church a tall
bell-tower
making a span of earth and sky,
a trinity of earth and craft and sky
as holy and almost as lovely
as any implacable blue.

But I remember better —
though stone outlast us, I can still hear —
a small goatherd singing
in a high, thin, clear voice,
half-Gregorian but more blithe,
on the opposite hill across a dry
riverbed, his black goats meandering.
He'd be in his thirties now, let's hope.
Let's hope.

The riverbeds go dry, the fountains climb,
the warm colours grow.

Amhrán na mBréag

In the middle of the wood I set sail
as the bee and the bat were at anchor just off shore
I found in the sea's rough shallows a nest of bees
In a field's ear I saw
a mackerel milking a cow
I saw a young woman in Greece boiling the city of Cork
   over the kitchen fire
Last night, in a serpent's ear, I slept sound
I saw an eel with a whip in her hand whipping a shark
   ashore
MacDara's Island told me he never saw more wonders:
a kitten washing a salmon in the river
the music-mast of a ship being
conceived in a cat's arse
a badger in the nest of an eagle milking a cow
and a sparrow wielding a hammer putting a keel on a boat.

after Micheál Mharcais Ó Conghaile

Driscoll 5: Glories Clear

A woman went to Stephen's Green, taking her three sons, to meet a nine-year-old boy, close friend of her son his age. They waited, as arranged, by the pond in the Green, where the beautiful ducks are fed or stoned. In the Green, where twenty years before Driscoll had seen black be beautiful and blond be beautiful together, seen

> miscegenation make its glories clear.

They waited by the summer pond, to go with that boy, their friend, to Bewley's Oriental Café for a summer treat: cool milkshakes, iced coffee, cakes. They waited for half-an-hour, three-quarters, gave him up, left; and as they came out the Arch, there the boy was waiting, near the mobile X-Ray unit, near help, so they went and had the treat but after a time he came out with it, why he'd not waited inside the Green, by the peaceful water, not kept exactly the appointed place, the beautiful incomparable safety, the irreplaceable warmth, of a definite appointment with friends: 'I didn't want to go in alone,' he said, 'they call me "nigger"; when I go in with you' (he turned to her son his age, his friend) 'they're afraid to say it but when I go in alone . . .'

> to Stephen's Green, where
> ignorance makes its miseries clear.

Two days later, brooding on this, Driscoll, grey in the face as always, entered a telephone-kiosk on Stephen's Green, opposite Emmet, who died for freedom, his cool green lissome strength, his vibrant stone challenge, a stone's throw from the College of Surgeons, the Hippocratic oath, help — and the first thing he saw, on the pale-grey inner wall of the kiosk was, in exquisite lettering, in rich bright black: 'Dirty nigger whore'.

The boy is nine, now. An Irish woman gave him birth. It could be, it was meant to be, his Green.

He's only nine, now. What danger will become? Of him? Of
those mocking schoolchildren? well schooled . . .

This happened in Dublin
        to a child.
This happened in a capital city
        in the '70s.
In sunlight, in summer,
        by water, near trees.
This happened
        among children
        to a child.
The mindless make their glories clear.

Flames

A red setter leaping
constant up and down, up-and-down,
like a big, living flame
in a dark slum room
where an old poor woman lies in bed sick,
the heat cut off the light cut off,
her only light her only heat
the red-gold setter leaping
tireless up and down like a tall
sinuous brilliant almost healing flame.

Never such buoyancy, never!

A long skinnymalink with auburn hair
loose-limbed in his mid-thirties
immaculate in a flame-coloured suit,
leaping up and down, up-and-down,
like a loose-haired flame
in a bar at the head of the Zeedijk
at one in the morning as Justin
played planxties on the penny-whistle.
Such Amsterdancing! He couldn't get enough of it.
Vertical wavering, a grace, a flame.

Never such buoyancy, never!

Miracles

You were my last miracle, as I was your
miracle, though not your last,
no never your last, only one
of many, though for each of us your best.

Your generosity
taught me to counter jealousy, your feast
of gleaming white bread (rich black crust)
worked wonders, filled and blessed
my long emptiness.
I was hungry and you fed me.
I was dying and you raised me from the dead.

Miracles, though we have not been led to
believe it, are always done
by the one in need as well
as the one who harrows
both heaven and hell.

Had you been less lavish
    with your miracles,
I'd still be starving
    in the wilderness.

Though bittern and cormorant nest
in the ruins of your feast,
though the bitter beak tear my breast
that cannot forget
your gleaming, sheltering breast,
we stole fire together
from hell in a fennel-stalk:
you were my last
miracle, and my best.

morning, September 1981

Findrum

Findrum:
the same room:
6 a.m.
10 years later, and I am
still here,
sitting in a similar
though not the same
armchair,
and not gazing
at you naked
asleep on the bed
nor waiting
but only staring
at an empty, sagging bed.

Oh for you to be here
and we could sag it more:
even break it
right down to the floor!

To Maria Spiridonovna on Her Keeping

To Maria Spiridonovna on her keeping
in the hungry Moscow of 1920
a friend brought
                        eggs and cherries.
I'd love to know what colour they were:
white eggs and black cherries,
brown eggs and red cherries —
or duck-blue?
'Who's for duck-blue cherries?'

Does it matter what colour they were?
It matters everything,
                        and not at all.

One of the country-people Maria had spent years in jail for
    under the Czar
smuggled to her in hiding, in gratitude,
when she was nearly starving,
hiding from the betrayers of the revolution,
eggs and cherries to eat.
One of those country-people who'd smuggled letters to her
    from many parts of Russia,
asking her to tell them if this new October Christ
had so soon been crucified again,
smuggled to Maria in her need
eggs and cherries to eat.

And Maria smuggled them into the knapsack of her comrade
who was leaving on a dangerous mission
against the dictators who'd betrayed
the revolution, and Maria Spiridonovna, and black cherries,
    and the people.
Then she reached up to his tall arm
and stroked it.

He went on his mission, let's hope the danger gave him time
to find those eggs, those cherries

dripping with love — with 'bourgeois sentimentality':
   so regrettably common
among the rustic proletariat, not yet made over,
among the deprived.
But does it matter? Whether he found them? Or what
   colour they were?
It used to matter before the dreams were broken:
the upstart bourgeois dream of safety —
the ancient human dream of freedom.

15 September 1978: Wexford

Dream

Cumbersome, the dream said, cumbersome.
What's the Gaelic for cumbersome? Find out,
   the dream commanded.
Somnambulist fingers hefted the huge new dictionary,
flicking the pages to the third letter:
coll, the hazel-tree, as the older lexicon told.
But cumbersome wasn't to be found in the new book,
even by fingers who thought themselves long accustomed.
A phleidhce! said the dream, exasperated,
'amadáin chríochnaithe! you call yourself literate
and you don't know yet that Kumbersome begins with a *K!*
K u m   b e r und so weiter.

So the fingers dread-fast in the dream scrabbled
in mild guilt for the letter *K,*
though somewhere in the back of their mind they had
   a resentful feeling
the letter *K* unlike the letter *V*
had never grown a Gaelic tree.
But scrabbling brought no news, no Kumbersome,
and suddenly it dawned on the fingers they were hunting
   an English word in an Irish-English dictionary
and it wasn't Ó Dónaill they needed at all but the other,
   darker blue
and somebody'd borrowed that blue and forgotten to give
   it back
so the fingers looked daggers at the dream,
or shrugged, or splayed,
and the dream let them off with a warning.

Leper-slit

Aluminium glinting faintly in a shuttered kitchen,
electric light switched off, the faint sun
stealing in — the antique shutters
don't quite meet —
that's what life can be like: a leper-slit,
what splendour! the eye could glimpse
only part of — the sermon's paunch, not lips,
but listen — could lepers hear? unglazed the slit let
thin billows of incense out (could the leper-king smell,
or choke on peace, who never choked on war,
or choke on talk of peace?)

Are we all kings? All lepers? All both?
One day the leper fitting his yearning to the narrow bright
    groove,
his azure hands on either side clutching the gargoyle stone,
met another darkling eye: the lonely, bored parson
mad to escape the drafty, crampt chapel
into the wide leprosarium,
the kingly outside world:
the porch, too sanctified, no exit,
the stained glass unbreakable,
sacrilege a man-trap or makeshift —
only the thin leper-window could let him out —
could his billowing soul fit,
like incense, through? Each gaze
recoiled, then the leper let go of the gargoyles,
and rolled around in stitches on the grass;
the parson rolled in the nave; but he was more
of a gargoyle than the leper,
and he'd glimpsed what was left of regal
in the leprous gaze — here
the chronicle breaks off (the stubborn scriptorium
no doubt invaded by even more civilized barbarians,
a tiny golden yearling pocketed, habit hitched up in a
    scurry),
eras later, bulldozer found

adhering to the sides of the leper-slit
shreds of a soul — soiled silk;
in the nave, crushed elderberries,
and wound around the gargoyle's ear
a charm against the plague.

But lepers have been known to ring
their bells against the belfries,
and when at last I folded back the antique shutters
they creaked, peeled, muffled
for a moment the leaking roof, the sun poured in,
not faint; I put the aluminium on for tea,
the apple-tree was at last in full flower,
and the leper-slit, a fossil theory, divine right,
lay in the grass among bright-yellow weeds,
lower than a snake in a waggon-track, awaiting
its own antarctic truck.

Orgy

'Let's go somewhere else and have an orgy'
you said with a happy smile to the other five of us
holding an Irish kaffee-klatsch in a corner of that good party
which had not yet risen to kissing.
You were in your mid-twenties and the other four
were in their teens or early twenties — divine ages all —
and I was already four years beyond
that decade when some idiot claimed,
with a drowning man's grasp on a grain of truth,
life begins. Given precocity in the one divine activity
where I never was given it I could have fathered the five of
        you.
So I looked at the joy and the loving amusement on the
        beautiful young faces
believing there was more love and longing between us than
        trouble and I longed to say 'Yes',
but I had to say: 'You're all young and I'm not'
and that exasperated your generous heart so you said:
'For Christ's sake, you're young!'
so I accepted it not as a drowning man but as one learning
        to swim.

As it turned out the orgy never happened,
we just went on joking and getting drunker and drunker
        right where we were,
and looking at maddening pictures and going a little madder
        than before
but your exasperated generosity
kept me younger for weeks.

The Poet Rides on Horseback through the Night

for Francis Devine

Not flautist but flute-player
not violinist but fiddler
or, if you must,
fiddle-player

      Paddy Rambles through the Park.
      The poet rides on horseback through the night.
      Were you there when they crucified my Lord?

Flute-player not flautist
not Northern Ireland but the Six Counties
not the Maze but Long Kesh
not itinerant but traveller
singing or mending or selling
or drinking too much and breaking heads
just like the rest
and often keeping faith — to music and stories —
the rest would never know
or not have kept.

      Were you there when Amos Barton
      struck up the Flogging Reel? Did you see
      the Fiddler Doyle mount
      the Black Mare of Fanad, to hear
      sea-music? Were you there the night
      Rosario played the Bunch of Grapes
      in the Holly Bush?
      And Trollope in the corner read
      The Eccentricities of Cardinal Pirelli?

Not Europe but the Common Market
though half the world now calls it Europe
as though the vast horror and glory and all the art

of Europe could be so
shrunk down . . .

  Were you there when Darach Ó Catháin sang
   in a pub in Leeds?
  and the barman said 'We'll have no Pakistani
   music here'
  and Darach's black hair
  glowed blacker still . . .

Not Great Britain or the U-nited Kingdom
but England: where hungry women
bore bread and blood on a pike,
where Kilvert
watched the fields, where Hudson met
Moses Found, and saw
starling hiding among the sheep, and I saw
near Ripon plover among the sheep.

  Were you there when Militrissa Kirbityevna
   lilted
  Welcome-home-dear-husband-however-drunk-
   you-be
  for Koba on his keeping, little knowing . . .

Not America but — some smaller, better name.
Such size may never learn
any small, beautiful name.
But even they might lose their name
when they ride the last big aeroplane,
so not America but Las
Americas.

  Were you in the Plover when Paddy Taylor
  struck up The Magpie on the Gallows
  and then
  The Rose Revised?

Paddy Rambles through the Park
we ride on termites through
all but the darkest night.

Affection

Once my name was Clais an Mhictíre
Wolf Hollow
but calling me out of my name they miscalled me
Clashavictory
From hideous murderous clash
                                   their victory came
their thoughts ran wild on victory
Clais an Mhictíre — my old name wantoned
earth and animal slain
conquest-gloating

And my name was
                        Beig-Éire
Little Ireland
The people who gave me that name
knew affection and fun
                        as well as desecration
But the ignorant invaders calling me out of my name
their tongues bloated with conquest
reduced Beig-Éire
to Beggary
          Island
as the whole island — all Éire Mhór —
was beggared, and is beggared in the mind:
the glade-scriptoria desecrated,
latrines paved
with tiles from a synagogue,
the hands of music
                      cut off in sport.

Burnham Deepdale

Once in a dark porch in Burnham Deepdale
we looked at a very small stained-glass window
at human level, you could touch it:
The Sun, not afraid to come in.
A big round, golden, beaming face,
filling the whole small space of glass,
blazing away merrily, lighting and warming,
not scorching — mo bhrón géar! —
the blighted clay, the drúchtín crushed . . .

That big, round, golden, beaming face
more beautiful than Blake,
Palmer's apple-orchard etching,
shone, eight centuries young.
The Armagh apple-orchards too
have bloomed eight centuries beneath
an Iron Crow's claws.

That small, vast sunniness enclosed in dark stone
under the infinite, serene, sequent, billowing
clouds of Norfolk,
the highest skies in Europe —
hot yellow glass sunbursting the tomb —
glowed at human level, arm's reach;
but the Five Grey Sisters cannot be touched,
are out of us, are higher than any benign
friendly Norfolk heavens, they lour, iron-grey,
battleship-bleak, they rule the waves of pity,
they outstare
Barnsley Main Seam.
Eternity's filled their tall, shoulderless, hipless,
narrow straightness, with silencers,
but they make an ugly noise like helicopters
over the green garth of Derry,
over the apple-orchards . . .

So how can folk whose very breath
is continuity ever understand
us whose breath is broken, whose old gold glass
they've broken, made us break,
make us break still?

The drúchtín trampled under conquering hoofs,
the maiden broken, her May broken,
the searching girl her sweet cheat gone,
her drúchtín lost, the dew undone —
that gentle rain — the springtime and the altars
broken as if for ever,
no glass-painters left even in Blandford —

What might altars matter, could the girl find again
her little white slug in a green garth on a May morning?

Is the continuity merely a papering-over,
an endless combat-jacket?
sang-froid just a strait-jacket?
Does Ermin Street run crooked after all?

But in Burnham Deopdale — spell it right —
the sun was full on,
it glowed like the Book of Kells or butterbrot,
as if no iron crows had ever scratched
the face of summer, it shone full
on the white back of her little drúchtín
before the cavalry came down, on the dead face
of a young girl mar thug sí féin
an samhradh léi go deo.

Clear the Stove in the Morning

for Mícheál MacGarry

Clear the stove in the morning
like clearing the decks for action
last night's goulash now congealed, faintly
distasteful, empty
the teapot, rinse, clear the stove for action.

The water boils, take down the caddy, place
its lid upon an unlit jet, unlid
the teapot, where to put it? place
one lid upon the other, speed
is all, the water's going off the boil —

The teapot-lid entirely hides
the other: it might as well not be there
suddenly it's *not* there
and that reminds the morning potterer
of an early-summer garden
a whole year back:

Door-bell rung twice, no answer, the friend not in,
walk down the short path, between the narrow grasses,
that faint suburban sadness when a door in sunshine
fails to open, then halt: the eye caught suddenly
by something covered, something covering:
on a dandelion, a butterfly!
Now you see it, now you don't!
Human, creep close; quiet; watch:
the red-and-brown creature, wings wide,
as if suspended, motionless, an inch above the grass,
completely hiding the flower — looknohands!
a bit like a boy on a bike — still,
a flutterby not moving?
wait — intruder, leave;
but once outside the railing, glance back:

the butterfly is still there,
held in air,
the yellow still invisible,
that small space between membrane and grass
resembling a mystery — go home and put the kettle on;
    remember.

Flowering Stump

The stump of an apple-tree breaks into flower
against a prison-grey wall.
Trapped in speculation's path, what up to now
was a fine full tree, bearing fruit
forbidden to me but not to children,
was by the builders left
three stumpy arms,
half its old height.
From childhood I could almost box that fox
just by leaning out the window, can anyone see now,
crossing the morning grass that vulpine ghost,
grey as a jail wall? for eight months
I've kept the curtains closed against the building noise next
    door,
the sight and stench of a dross calf enthroned,
for a month, noise at an end, kept them closed
against the new grey wall
dull matt menacing almost as bad as a prison wall,
prisoning away from me the gentle curve
of Dublin hills I lived with since a boy,
the grey stone mass permits
no near tree, no far hills —
these three pitiful stumps the hackers left
are not a tree — but now!
how can I keep the curtains closed against
these brave white flowers!
Three small blossoms, a few green shoots
on the lowest, nearest stump;
three days later,
the high stump flowers,
next day the third as well is green and white,
it's truly as if the tree is telling me,
telling its mutilators,
telling the prisoned, imprisoning builders,
telling all demolishers and all money:
You haven't killed me yet.
You can't kill me — yet.

Morning after morning, for a brief season,
morning after morning, fox-ghost forgotten,
I open curtains, for big windows thankful,
and watch the green and the white,
the tender green, the vivid white,
waving in front of a prison wall,
breaking the prison,
breaking into and out of that prison,
demolishing it for me for a brief season.

For a brief while we wait, in vain, for fruit,
green lasts longer than white,
who knows what new destruction another year may bring,
who knows what fresh fruit?
Like living things the darker-grey shadows
of coloured leaf and twig
move in the sunny breeze across the pale-grey wall
demolishing, enhancing, building,
re-building hope

Bright Red Berries

Bright red berries, bright-dark-red,
thronged in a small tree's dullish green,
between the women's convenience
and the brand-new Luxury Apts.

The small tree is still there,
it brings forth its berries against
the dull dark-red prison brick,
the grey monoglot piss.

It used to survive behind railings,
on a narrow patch of drab grass and empty cans,
behind it prouder trees and a proud house.

Luxuriant bulldozers ground
the house down, grass out, grew
bijou brick barbarity.
But still the tree stands, by grace of greed.
The gloomy belvedere maws must
have more than convent and garage
to mint-julep at.

Beside the broken footpath, a small tree still brings
colour and fruit forth

Bad Milk

Four-days-half-solid, the milk,
held over the sink, is loath:
it bucks and gouts
under my hand urging,
chugging, the squat bottle:
thick blobs of curdle, thrawn
to block —
my hand sees again
the stricken mammoth head down,
tongue out, the big dark neck
straining, convulsed; coughing,
slow, painful, out
onto the sand the gouts of blood.

A True Story Ending in False Hope

for Martin Collins

The barman vaulted the counter
landing with a fine clatter
beside our musical table;
he nearly upset the pints
of all the dominical couples.
'We'll have no music here,'
he roared, bursting a blood-vessel.
We weren't, in fact, a steel-band,
or a demolition-squad,
so Justin gestured the tin-whistle
towards the married couples:
'Does anyone mind this
                       music?'
Some said they didn't,
the rest sang dumb,
but one old woman spoke up loudly:
'We like it,' she cried,
'it brightens things up a bit here.'
The barman burst another vessel.
'Out! Out!' he shouted.
'We'll finish our drink,' said the Corkman,
the Corkman who'd *asked* for the music,
and we did,
but we left —
uttering suitable imprecations.

We crossed the unmusical road,
skirting a public jax
that hadn't yet turned into a ghost,
boarded a chopper for heaven,
and played and drank till closing-time,
thinking how musical
Ireland
      will
         be.

Traffic-lights are Dangerous

The cars mount the pavement, break the lights
which don't last long enough: old people just about
make safety, the cars break the lights, raid the footpath
right outside the barracks, a squad-car
zooms out at once to catch the culprit
through night parks of dread
(it does an' my Nobel Prize).

I make it safe home, and climb the stairs
to borrow sugar from an old
old woman, there's an apple-segment
in among the sugar:
                    to keep it dry, she says.

The lout leaps out, from his big shiny car,
and tells the man he's nearly killed:
'You take my number; right?
And I'll get you.'
The rip-off republic cherishes OK

I climb the stairs to borrow tea,
there's orange-peel nestling in the caddy,
'I'm all fruit,' she says.

You toucha my car: I breaka your neck,
one sticker grates — and to think that we thought,
in '45, the war was fought
against that kind of bullshit.
Shift your ass, another windscreen screams —
it's a wonder they can see to drive . . .

I climb the carpet, the leaking roof
has washed one step quite bright,
and hear the old old woman
singing to her windowsill ring-doves
in a high, young girl's voice.

Manifest Destiny

That every county in this developed state
sprout its very own
Ballyporeen: stone-crop, small potato, jackstone.
That's a must, a summit priority.
The tourist bounty, the NATO fall-out,
could solve — dissolve — the Border overnight.

With small-potato-lounges in every single county,
wouldn't the tyrant be proud of us?
He wouldn't even have to murder us.
Next time he calls
let's all
crawl
on naked knees and one hand — the other
tugging green plastic forelocks (there's a thought
for the IDA) — to as near as we can get to the Dáil,
our Dáil,
our, the people's, parliament,
and beg his majesty, this highest king,
via petitions clampt in our gums or green plastic teeth,
signed by all five thousand million
inhabitants of this developed state,
to let us become the fifty-second
state of the union — if any uppity rainbow
dares to show itself higher than this most ardest rí,
why shucks we'll shoot it down,
lower than a snake in a waggon-track,
with missiles the milk-thief lent us —

And speaking of her, we might as well while we're at it
petition for re-admission to the Empire —
no not the commonwealth or common poverty
the old Empire itself, for nothing less
can satisfy
our plastic forelocks.
We thus could be
ruled by three

which is much better
than one-and-a-half.

But for all this glory to come to pass
we must work night and day
might and main
to ensure
that every future incumbent of the White House
can, with cross-channel help,
trace his glorious descent back
to one or other manifest destiny village in the ould sod.
It is of course just possible
that some Chicano, Black, or Jew
might throw a bleeding-heart spanner in the works,
paint the white house black or even rainbow-coloured.
The danger is remote; but should it happen,
after the button's pressed, and we're all born again,
that need not faze us, we can always find,
even for black or jew or nicaragüense,
a touch o' the shamrock, a drop a' the oul' crater,
the ever-new volcano — the Limerick pogrom
and the Sack of Baltimore might yield
some helpful hints . . .

Climbing High

When a man can't say sorry to another
though he knows full well he should
when a man can't apologize to another
though he *knows* he *should*
when he can't spare
two syllables
or perhaps three an' a half
because it might, in court, be considered
an admission of liability
then we have climbed
into a plutocrat heaven
where *only* money talks

It always talked the loudest
even before it was born
but up to
not so long ago
some other hints got heard
at least they kept a flag flying
and through its tatters you could glimpse
once in a blue slump
humanity
and even that poor young eejit
once called Christ

But now that a man can't
say sorry to another man
though he knows full well he should
and only because of money
because of money only
then we're climbing high
on a gallows without end

The Lost Garden

I spoke to her as one child to another,
as the child I was
                        to the child she is,
as the child I remember, who is, remembering,
still here.
And, in part, she understood me.
As I, in part only,
understand.
I spoke to the child she still is,
and also, perhaps, to the woman she'll soon become.
I spoke to the child who plays in the garden I grew up in,
am not, now, allowed to enter;
can still — still —
watch.
Oh I spoke to the sweet-natured girl who can play there
to her heart's content,
for a while yet.
I spoke to the child,
in the mind only.

31 July 1983

Andalusia

At blazing, sweating lunch-time
the Andalusian building-workers erupted into the Catalan
    pub
downing work-dry litres of black dirt-cheap wine
guzzling their own big sandwiches but first of all erupting
six or seven at a time
down the three steps from the narrow street glare
into the officially cool Catalan shade;
some thought them noisy, others vital;
they cast their coins on the counter, making it ring!
looking the Catalan publican straight in the eye
as much as to say, We're as good as you,
and we can prove it
                    in your own lousy terms.

The day they got their first helmets —
for capital was beginning to pretend to possess a
    conscience —
they came leaping down into the quiet place
leaping and japing and juggling their helmets in the winey
    air
green helmets and yellow helmets and red
stript to the burning waist and loving the bright colours on
    their heads
and not ashamed of it, and not ashamed.

The Catalan binmen, in their yellow costumes,
balancing wickerwork stench upon their heads,
like Andalusian women balancing the glinting water,
weren't all that staid either,
they made a game of garbage.

A Colour Photo

for Piero and Ariella

Melita came from Italy bringing barmbrack from Bewley's
aromatic and warm still when she opened the cake-box
   on the round black table,
they were just bringing the first batch up the stairs from
   the bakery
when she walked into the shop that morning
so she got the first brack of the day
and came straight to me: on the round black
table we'd worked at together so often
the brack in its open box was breathing, warm, knobbly,
   blackish and brown, just crusty enough,
we went to work the better for it

O Ariella
her mother at seventy dancing with you in a summer
   garden
her dying face alight with love and happiness
her long red gown glowing and swirling to match
the glowing grass and the darker lustre of branches
and your white frock and auburn curls
and laughter one year old!

And us, in the north, in March, looking at such
halcyon, heart-breaking, death-defying pictures,
and eating the warm cake your mother brought me

Will you remember when you grow
dancing with your granny on the grass between the trees
a month before she died, her beautiful dying face
alight with love for you and love for life,
knowing she was dying but happy to be with you, her
   daughter's child,
dancing with you in that last summer,
dancing for all your summers

A Memory of Belfast in 1974

for Caoimhe Ní Dhuibhinn

The towering menace-aforethought
imperial-metal contraption the people named
Silver City no sheepswool stuck
in its high wire that Sunday morning,
and the warm sky wasn't bleeding.
But under the menace, on the grass,
children were playing.
Some o' them swinging on new bright-coloured swings,
swinging right up to the sky,
their small feet almost reaching Silver City,
almost toppling it down.

It wasn't the Sabbath-authorities put the swings there,
but the Lord's Day did its bit to barb the wire.

Three of us strolling, that sunny morning,
it nearly felt like peace.

Then we were stopped for questioning.
Nowt serious, it didn't last long,
but as we resumed our stroll
the oldest of us said:

'I'm 61.
I was born in this city,
I've lived here all my life,
an' I can't go for a walk on a Sunday morning
without being stopped by a British soldier.'

The sun was dazzling on Silver City
as back we strolled for Sunday dinner,
the swings were still — the kids
must all have gone home for theirs.

Before we got back to his house
he stopped and said to me:
'We're a betrayed people' —
looking me straight in the eyes,
like a Cree Indian telling it like it is
to the soi-disant-white camera:
'We're a betrayed people.'

Later we sat drinking beer in the back garden.
The helicopters with their ugly blurting
only attacked the blue sky
every fifteen minutes,
but at times they came quite low.

The Right to Love

for Mairéad Looby

A young woman in the Bogside went out walking
with a British Tommy, so the freedom-fighters
tarred-and-feathered her — before that torture
did English conscript and Irish girl make love?
go the whole hog? let's hope they did
for what's it to anyone whether or no
's goidé sin don té sin nach mbaineann sin dó
but the freedom-fighters said it was
their business, called her a risk, a threat
but her mother cried out:
Wee girls have a right to love!
crying out from her heart
who was once a wee girl herself
crying out from her loving heart
for all the world to hear
crying out to a world of love beyond
even her own people's agony and hope
even beyond her own, but yet within
all such hope, all suffering —
her shriek of hope
making its dogged, quiet way
through all the conventional, fashionable,
holier-than-thou, halfways-liberal newsprint
to lovers everywhere,
to pity poor lovers everywhere:
Wee girls have a right to love.

She Fell Asleep in the Sun

'She fell asleep in the sun.'

That's what they used to say
in South Fermanagh
of a girl who gave birth
unwed.

A woman from Kerry told me
what she'd always heard growing up was
leanbh ón ngréin:
a child from the sun.

And when a friend of mine from Tiernahilla
admired in North Tipperary
a little lad running round a farmyard
the boy's granda smiled:
'garsúinín beag mishtake'.

A lyrical ancient kindliness
that could with Christ accord.
Can it outlive technolatry?
or churches?

Not to mention that long, leadránach,
latinate, legal, ugly
twelve-letter name not
worthy to be called a name,
that murderous obscenity — to call

any child ever born
that excuse for a name
could quench the sun for ever.

Let's Hope

A girl and her child
extinct in a field.
A boy got beaten to death in a park.
They didn't mean to kill him.
They live.
His family say he wasn't.
Nobody meant to kill her.
One morning last year
from the top deck of a bus
I saw the living sunlight flooding
trees and grass in Fairview Park
with light, life, splendour —
as if no death,
as if no hate,
as if no ignorance ever.
Perhaps that very same morning filled
her field of death with glory —
even love: some sort.
Whether he was or not, let's hope
he enjoyed whatever it was,
or just himself, before
they taught themselves
no lesson soon enough.
Let's hope Ann Lovett knew,
before that fear, some joy.

Until

een fenster is alles
　　　　　　— Paul van Ostaijen

The way an old man from his window looks out at the beauty
　of nature
　　　grass, trees, creatures
　　　　the beauty surviving the horror
is not the same way that a young man
　looks out the window and goes out the door and enters
his own full nature and every nature and goes on living them all
　crushed insect, predator's prey: not surviving, not surviving
but the young man still living it all
　living it up and living through it all
　　dancing or crawling every minute of it until
　　　he sits looking out of a window

Snowflake

for Richard Riordan

Snowflake in a spider's web
sycamore-leaf in a bay-tree.

Filament clung to the back
window for days that winter,
keeping the snowflake, never
a spider in sight, each morning
for days I looked and still
the snowflake held in the web
as pure a white
as when it first came down —
all other snow
well gone — then rain
washed away that flake.

From a tall tree last autumn
one tawny leaf wind-crossed
the front garden, came to rest
in close-clustering dark-green
bay just under a window
unseason sheltering season
for a few days. For days:
the big, five-point, mottlegolden
leaf in dark-green held
while sycamore-leaf upon leaf
went underfoot in grass.

Bringing back
a snowflake.

May 1989

An Empty House

The small sycamore
invading the bird-house
thrusting those
unmistakable, beautiful
big leaves
into the kennel-like
dark emptiness
the birdless
even crumbless
blank space
filling
with living
green.

The bird-house
began in the back.
No birds entered,
though once a tiny
bird with a blue tail
alighted on
the roof a split
second. Shunted
to the front garden —
less cat-risk —
the bird-house
still failed.

Soon again
the small invading
tree will be
trimmed back,
the desolate kennel
still ignored
by small birds
feeding on the grass.

Saturnino

for Jürgen Dierking

Hurling the frail door wide open, erupting down
from dim-lit narrow side-street three shallow steps
into the dark, small, quiet pub the raw young marine
in dark blue blared
'Is there nobody here?'
where Ernie and I were percht on stools at the counter
getting slowly sozzled conversing with Saturnino
the half-tipsy publican from León
who didn't know, just as well, what the gringo said
but Ernie knew exactly what the young lad meant
so 'Further down the Ramblas' he said gesturing lavishly,
his blond beard curling with amusement,
naming a dive where every sixth-fleet lecher
could rapidly get laid,
the lad scooted away
and Saturnino enquired: 'What did he say?'

When we told him, he got very angry:
we were the only three people in the pub,
but we were there
we were three
we were people
'Are we nobody?' he cried (though not in English)
rushing out along the narrow street
but came back fast from the Ramblas so loud and bright
Three brandies on the house, cheap rotgut stuff but still
'Are we not people?' he cried, at least three times
(at times only the literal
can express the imagination,
achieve any generous truth)
and then he erupted again in even greater anger
thinking of the women who'd have to be kind to that
    unthinking boy,
the women of his town, the women from all over Spain,
so he rushed to the door again and flung it wide

and cried into the narrow, dark, empty street:
'Con la gana que tienen
                          las pobres mujeres!
With the hunger they have — those poor women!
Con la *gana* que *tien*en
                          las *pob*res mu*jer*es!'
More than one of whom often
patronized his pub.
Drink was dirt-cheap in those days,
though the whores were beginning to get dear:
las pobres
                pobres mujeres
con la gana que tienen
con la gana those poor women
who were people
who were many
who were there.

Deprivation, Luxury, Envy

A man and a boy standing side by side
gazing into a cake-shop window
a posh Konditorei on a posh boulevard
the man lacking the money for even a cheap drink
who knows perhaps the boy could have bought the man
a glass of rotgut brandy
but a cake in that shop could cost the earth
the boy looked underfed not even enough lentils
let alone a posh cake.

Man and boy stood side by side for long minutes
without a word, the boy never once looking
at the man even out of the corner of his eye
The man wanted to say to the boy
I get paid next week I could buy you a few cakes
but he hadn't the courage so they went on standing there
side by side not speaking not making common cause
just eaten up with envy
the posh cakes eating their hearts away.

Then the boy walked off. And the man,
lacking the courage to break the window,
made for the nearest non-boulevardier bar,
where if the right member of the family was on
he might get a little more credit.

Even when at last he got paid
it wasn't to that shop the man went for cakes.
That city was chock-full of cake-shops.

Odessa

Called a Jew
six times:
once in middle age
five times in youth

Drunk Dublinmen
four times
as an insult
in pubs
but a courteous Dutchman
by water
in Haarlem

From '44 to '46
four times in Dublin pubs:
You're a Yid
   I'm not
You look like a Yid
    I'm not
You're a dirty Yid
    I'm not
    but I wish I was
You're a fuckin' Yid
    I am
    so what?

That last time
and the second-last
I was really frightened:
both men nearly hit me
only Dutch courage
(as a coward called it)
had at last made
indignation brave

One day in '52
walking in utter quiet

along the bank of a sunny canal in Haarlem
I lost my way
and bridge after bridge
not a soul in sight
no one even sitting on a stoep;
with a train to catch
I began to panic
then heaven sent
a very small old man
walking slowly in front of me

white hair, black suit,
small wizened face
not a word of English
he'd see me on my way
but he walked so slow!
Gij bent een Jied, he said
I knew that must be slang
but Why? said I
De baard, said he: the beard

After a pause:
There used to be thousands of them here
before the war
many in kaftans
The Germans took them away
After another pause:
They never did us any harm
not that I could see

Then our ways parted
I shook his hand and thanked him
I could have hugged him
I should have kissed and hugged him
hugged his frail old body
his true Dutch courage and courtesy

No one ever again called me a Jew
save that a Jewish friend in Leeds in '73
after six months of trust said:
I thought at first you might be Jewish
not because of your nose
but because of your lip — he smiled
so I smiled too, a trifle bravely
(and to think that my Seville Place father,
who spoke with affection of Odessa
and of Clanbrassil Street
used to call it a Hapsburg lip)

Those Dublin bowsies at the war's end,
all middle-aged, none well-heeled,
went for the nose not the lip.
That small old man in Haarlem,
by sunlit, peaceful water,
didn't look well-heeled either.

Ostfriesland

for Theo Schuster

1

I'm eating with four Germans
in a small East-Friesian town
magnificent Italian food.
Our host, a gallant man
who keeps on bringing out
books and records in the Nahsprachen —
tongues near to German —
for example: Plattdütsch.
And,
     for example,
             Yiddish.

He tells us, over
the sumptuous food,
there lives here now
only one Jew.
For a wild second I wonder
is it him?

Earlier, in his bookshop, leafing through
a history of this town,
I found a synagogue-photo.

Built in the 1880s. Burnt down,
like so many,
on Kristallnacht.

Now at the Italian table
I remember that small picture,
and wonder.
           But imagine it,
that one Jewish man

going back there, after the war —
after that war —
coming back (from where?)
coming back to what had been
his town too,
to make it, perhaps, his town again,
to be, in a way, alone there.

I fall silent, we all do
for a minute.
What right have I to wonder
or imagine?
Common humanity?
What right to assume it was ever
his town? Or doubt it?

2

One of these four I'm eating with
is the friend who brought me here,
a poet who has railed against and mocked
all hatred and savagery.
Two are sisters,
charming and beautiful,
who fed me as well as Italians could
on a balcony under the warm night
a week ago in Bremen.

I remember Elie Cohen the Dutch rabbi
telling the Dutch, after that war:
Don't think it couldn't happen here,
it could happen anywhere,
even in Holland.

3

Isroel
not ah but oh
not Israel but Isroel — that so
surprising vowel that unexpected *o*
sounding out clear on the LP sent — as good as his word —
to me in Bloom's town (whether his, or mine)
from a small East-Friesian town
sounding out in the rich prose
of a great storyteller Itschak Leib Peretz
in the rich voice
of Zvi Hofer
of the Institutum Judaicum
of Münster — Leib Peretz
who spoke with passion for Yiddish to be
the national tongue of the nation-to-be
                                        Isroel

Peretz
lost out to Hebrew, but on this record
made in Germany, not anywhere else,
his passion speaks again, his vivid zest,
all that humour and variety
which even goyim can tell (with the aid
of certain famous books) all that life
defying oppression, prejudice, all the narrowing forces,
abounds again, speaks Yiddish again, in Zvi
Hofer's abundant voice
as rich as Hebrew itself.

Winters

The old in winter
longing for the spring
hating the cold
longing for the first warm days
as if
wishing their lives away
even sooner

People at work
longing for pay-day
as if wishing
their lives away

People out-of-work
longing for dole-day
as if wishing —

And all wish
the very opposite:
more life, not less!

Workers
hating the 12-month winter
of low pay
The workless
hating their 12-month winter

The old in winter
shivering over heaters
longing for the spring

The horse lies
half out of the icy lake
its wings frozen

Barnsley Main Seam

for Peter Kiddle

Impeccable snow, eternally fresh, gold-clustering —
limitless icefield sparkled with golden igloos,
an ordered sprinkling, all mathematics
made sumptuous like the sound
of Ceva's theorem — the whole ceiling
so boundless a roof so soaring
as almost babellious in its worship,
                                    Vatican-voluptuous,
higher than God's own sky,
higher and whiter than even serenest
clouds over the Brecklands. Look! look up
at us, honey-knobs, pommes mousseline:
perfection of man's making —

Yet for-all-that a feast, a true, an even chaste
feast for spirit as for eye —
Stefansdom, Gaudí —
and for-all-that more accessible
to the tiny floored nape craning up
(like Čapek flat on his back in the pocked Alhambra)
than the Five Grey Sisters:
                                    grey-stained infinite-oblong glass,
austerest glass, how rich a grey,
an almost velvet grey, bleak brocade,
stuff so harsh hauteur
                                    you'd never want to stroke,
noli-me-tangere-vaginistic charm —
and flat on his back forever
the lissome silvery armour-body of young Prince William,
only thirteen, poor mite,
endless gazing sightless up
at buttertub slobs in a muslin-spud expanse,
no Amsterdancing prinsiade now for him,
his long grey slim steel as graced
as the five giant Sisters but him stretched

only one young boy, not five pious bayonets,
just one dead boy who never chose
to be born a prince but perhaps more easily
forgot he didn't
                    than
the miners who made the timber model
of Barnsley Main Seam

Not of high stone
not of deep coal
not of gold snow
nor grey glass
they built their small model
nestling modest into the minster wall:
'The Tribute of the Yorkshire Miners
to the Minster' —
or so it says and there the little model men are
not in sumptuous colours woven
not in bleak brocade
but well worked in wood
working away at the coal-face —

A hunk of white bread, spattered in blood,
and a black rag, aloft on a pike:
the hungry women of Honiton made their protest clear.
But that was in the bad old days, long before
enlightened centuries when the milk-thief drove
Derby and Merthyr Tydfil to hunger-strike.

Black white and red, those women planting a pike
in high gold-spattered snow
like a dominion flag in a polar icefield:
were *they* in the miners' minds when
they made
and gave
that blunt, matter-of-fact model of a pit-place,

dwarfed by antique splendour,
dwarfing splendour?

Were those riotous women and all the toiling mothers
of miners and masons and all the guilds and all
the muscle called unskilled
back to the tower of Babel and Brú na Bóinne
deep in the miners' minds? as though to say
to all that antique splendour (so buoyant still):
Men like us made you,
without us
you could not be.

Did Primitivo Pérez from
Where the Air is Clear
signing his name in the big book in the narthex
buying a minster minute
observe the miners' tribute, how
clear the sacred air must be
down pit?
Young miners flaunting shoulder-bags in the cage
grinning all over their glad eyes
ready for a prinsiade but
the old honey walls
of York are a different colour entirely —
and is there honey still for tea
in Honiton?
Or black bread, white faces, bad blood?

The Ghost of a Kiss

for Aogán Ó Muircheartaigh

The two warriors kissing at the ford
after massacring each other all day.
Doctors came with herbs to heal their wounds.
They broke bread together,
that sacred act.
Then they slept,
so as to go on fighting to the death.

At the end of the second day
they kissed again, halfway across the ford.
Which of them was Judas? which Christ?
They had been loving friends.
Herbs were brought. Bread broken.
They slept.

The third night
there was no kissing.
On the fourth day
one killed the other.

The ghost of Judas
cut himself down off his tree,
and ran to the hill to cut down
the ghost of Christ from his.
They embraced, and kissed again,
reliving that other kiss;
but now they had only each other to persecute,
only each other to betray.
They kissed, and started fighting to the death.

British Justice

for Paddy Joe Hill

For British
       read English.
For Justice
       read Law.

Koan

for William Cowper and Umberto Saba

Clearing a kitchen surface too long cluttered
you hear the sound
                    of spent matches
touching the handle of a silver spoon
a gentle tinkle
        you never heard
                that particular
sound before —
il mondo meraviglioso:
there's always a first time

Would unspent matches
lightly driven against
the handle of a silver spoon
make a different sound?

Legend

The Russian word for beautiful
is the Russian word for red.
The Chinese word for silk
is the Chinese word for love.

Beautiful red silk love.

Silk isn't always red —
is love always beautiful?
When you are with me,
yes.

Wouldn't I?

When I'm in your arms, do I think about death?
When I'm in your lovely young arms
I'm far too busy enjoying
being in your arms.
When I'm not in your arms or your company,
that fearful, despicable maniac still
crosses my mind now and then but
almost never stops me in my tracks
bleakly staring as far too often and long
in the ageing decade before
you took me by summer storm.
Let the stern shake their heads, I shan't
get my comeuppance any worse than them;
I never did think much of all
that Eros-Thanatos-inextricable
wisdom of ages. Hubris
has nowt to do with it, it's just
that love's about life not death,
I'm scarcely afraid any more —
tho' when it comes to the point and at my
age it could happen any minute — but in
the meantime and
three years next month is not too bad
as meantimes go though here I am
trying to thank you for this in particular and so
for the space of a poem ipso facto mentioning
the bully more often than usual, I wouldn't
go so far as to claim
you've made the wretch irrelevant
but it doesn't seem to matter so much any more,
love can
          work wonders.

Next Time I'll Measure Your Waist

You were so easy and fine last night I scarcely noticed
the homemade halo I'd brought,
rigged-up in a spare dream and you at first
were loath to wear — but I implanted it
firmly just as firm
                          as puritan childhood guilt —
tilt
remorseless tactfully off
your soft black hair

Until you stopped me snoring
                          ('gently', you said gently)
so then I leant across you, nearly falling over,
to look, too eager, under the bed for that ring to snatch
back
but it must have melted into the thin ichor
of a spare dream and when you dredged me back
I never missed that half-unreal halo
for the real ring had all its wits about me,
your kind strong body filled us both.

Wooden Hoops for Iron

When Edward Thomas was a child in Wandsworth in the
   Eighties
boys bowled iron hoops
girls
     bowled
         wooden
Were little boys, when iron
fell upon their little bare legs,
better able to stand it?
Erich Fromm, on the other hand,
placed the end of matriarchy at around 1300 BC
Before that date did boys and girls both
bowl wooden hoops?
Or girls iron
       and boys wooden?
Some have asserted
the real human rot set in
with the iron age

Delicate wrought-iron balconies
The Gaudiesque torch-extinguishers on a Bath crescent:

But climbing a wooden stile near Saggart
on a now rainy now sunny day
Climbing a wooden stile

But when the Sun was Shining

Too long now since
he stood at the side of a country road,
facing the bushes, watching —
a boy again —
the golden or silver jet
ascending, arching, toppling,
sunlit against no not against but on
the vast blue sky
and then as he fastened up his eyes took in
the whole green countryside
all Ireland his, and every traveller's —

but back to the waiting friends in the patient car
and away again west or south
it wasn't such fun when it rained
and hefted you couldn't wait till the next pub
so facing barbed wire or bushes gone dull
you just let it drizzle
not soaring not sunlit, though even then
if the rain too was only drizzle a small
whiskey-bottle you could raise — for even in rain
it shone — up to the skies in defiance,
forgiveness, gratitude, hope

for a break in the distant clouds,
more gorse the further south,
but when the sun was shining that was best,
and you were jetting silver, toppling gold,
claiming the whole green country free to enjoy

February 1992

Sparrowthorn

Remember, Kate, when Sparrowthorn was nearly built
you took me round
                    the already attractive house,
and in the bare oblong guest-room-to-be, a bird,
as we stood there halfway
                            between two window-frames
not glazed yet, swiftly flew
                            in-past-us-out, so fast
we barely caught the colour I declare was blue
a plump small bird that for a second flashed
over the bare boards
                        between the bare walls, to clothe
as fabric later — soon — the bare air: a warning
or welcome; who can tell? or no meaning at all
but a blessing, meant or not, as we stood there in the warmth
of friendship and your excitement at this growing home
where children now have grown —
                                how well the bird got through
before the glazier came

early summer, 1989

The Vale of Clara

for Seán and Rosemarie Mulcahy

When the man through the wire fence looked in
   at the young deer beneath the trees
(stopped by its dappled beauty) the surprisingly small animal
   looked at him over its shoulder, then high-stepped away
      out of sight —
how admiration even across so perfect
   a difference can frighten beauty; the man, wondering
whether to feel faintly guilty, christening
   that scruple fatuous, walked along to the gate into the wood.
The trees met high over his head, he walked through, in peace.

Till from the path-side, by his quiet but not quiet enough
   progression disturbed a brace of pheasants clattered
up, clattered away above him, such a loud mad metal
     clattering
   the man was even more frightened than the small young
   deer.
He stood still for a minute or two, then not high-stepping
   stepped along regardless.
A narrow, winding stream came down the slope nearly to
    the path
   its own path faltered by small stones like small weirs, the
   brown
bogwater glinting, flitting in the leafy sunlight,
   the small brown or fawn translucent bubbles forming,
    lingering,
quenching, at the huge pebbles' dalliance —

Three or four bubbles in a tight cluster reminding
   the man of sloe-berries dark bloom but not much
    glistening
on a slanting bush on a high hill overlooking Glendalough
   climbed up that same September day the dark berries
reminding him then of halfway up that hill sidestepping the
   tight-clustering bright black

sheep-leavings glinting up the hill to the glory of God the
    Sun.

Bright, light-brown, small water-globes in a wood — the
    townie
  looked from the high hill down at the round tower
in the pure centre of the valley, ringed — how unerring
    their choice
  but more meaning for him the visible world
over to the right, off-centre, in the pure middle of a rich
    meadow
  a spreading oak or elm — school never toyed with
    nature —
that big tree alone in the centre of a square field.

That big, enduring tree as lovely as all the small
  brief bubbles on a hidden, small wood-stream. This man
    went back
deer-haunted, pheasant-scared, self-scared, contented, cured,
  to the bridge-house of his friends who had given him
that day.

A Wooden Stile

for Garret and Stephen

A wooden stile near Saggart
a now rainy now sunny day
the stile spanned a gate
into the beckoning forest
the small boys climbing over
soon disappeared in the trees
neither one lingered
but the man did
the man who climbed with such
un-boyish care
a few, wet, stile-steps

And then he turned his back on the forest,
turning slow, so
careful not to slip on the wet wood
and looked across at the land sloping away
down to the city and the sea
the lights just beginning to come on

The boys were still in the trees, the man
went on standing on top of a stile and looking.
He knew at last from his care he was middle-ageing
but he didn't care at all — well hardly at all —
for there he was standing on top of a stile and looking
down from as good as a hilltop, if not better —
a wooden stile so simple and clever a man-made thing,
nature and human at ease together, the man would soon
filled with joy but gingerly
descend the four wet steps

And cross the road to his old friends' car,
their two small sons come back from the trees,
and all drive home in friendship.

Font Romeu

You were the burning bush in a barn church,
you were a redsetter leaping
inside my darkest room,
you were never the small faint violet
naked light-bulb in a third-class
hard-bench carriage in a snail-pace train
inside the darkest night, malodorous impossible to read by,
but more the cool green light of a late summer
along the clear-cut sierra the following evening,
your quick saw cut away my lumbering pointless wood,
you were the brightest light on the highest snow at Font
    Romeu,
all my three-tense life
spread out and calming down from that high point:
under your hot-blue naked sky from you, my Pyrenees —
you were never the Cliffs of Moher for I could scale you
but more like the whitest foam the sumptuous dark-green sea
down there at the base of the cliff when I was young,
you were never a little white fishbone
prised out of my throat and shining in the penumbra
of an oto-rhino-laryngologist's room the blinds half-drawn
against the unbearable street-heat-light outside,
for you are as neat and far more fair
than even that small white bone and I can swallow you,
I can walk up all your avenues, can bear your heat, your
    light,
you were the healing water gleaming
in a low-slung, entirely unroman aqueduct
above a dry white-grey riverbed,
you were that sudden red blaze of tomatoes
in one small field in Los Gallardos
in an endless waste of sick-silver esparto famine-dust
where it hadn't rained for eight years,
you were as succulent as Pyrenean pigeon-in-cabbage,
you were the green trees filling the big plain windows —
no lush stained-glass to keep nature out —
of a strictly colourless Hebridean kirk

you were as sudden and rich as the summer trees
breenging in the window the plain pews
pell-mell with rich green leaves
you were the burning bush in a barn church you were and are
all the places I ever travelled to, only truer, only human,
and all the places I never travelled before,
you were the light unerring of the god of youth and love
breaching my darkest cave at the winter solstice.

Pulcherrima Paradigmata

'The sopranos are hard men':
proclaimed in large white
block letters
on a Harcourt St pavement
in the mid-forties:
it lasted for days

In certain dialects of Galician
the word for sister
is the word for brother

'You know,'
said the Virgin Queen
to the Keeper of the Tower,
'that I am Richard the Second'

The Irish
for stallion
is feminine

And as Florence Nightingale
wrote to her Queen,
'I have slept
with some of the finest
women in England.'

Yet Another Reason for Writing in Irish

'He'
is cold,
hard,
weak.

'She'
is warm,
soft,
strong.

An Early Fifties Contrast between the Giudecca and Wexford Street

A tall skinny old woman in a crumpled black-drab
dress right down to her ankles
dancing slow gyrating very slow
all by herself in a big snug
to no music except her own
and all by herself bar me
to no music except the music in her own
head of skimpy every-which-way
grey-white hair

    The long, dull, black dress,
    crumpled,
    I can still see it swaying
    can still see her long, thin,
    utterly pale face,
    flaccid,
    the long thin nose of it,
    the small dark sharp eyes dancing,
    the lively slow swaying
    seventy years of her.

A skinny, less than tall
young man in a drab, crumpled
black smock behind a counter
in a cheap, rudimentary bar,
all by himself when I came in,
his utterly pale, pinched face
shocking in that adriatic summer
between black smock and red, redsetter hair,
his eyes less lively in his twenties
than that old woman's but just as full as hers
but filled with pain and yearning

    Small talk, three glasses, growing
    unspoken sad-eyed friendship,

'come back tomorrow', but when the young
foreigner went back — behind the counter
only the big brother tough as nails
his dark hair dull his black
smock not crumpled, clean — as hate or pride.

1991

Enriqueta Bru

Everything about her was neat,
and, be sure, still is:
small bones, neat features,
trim figure in trim garb,
fair-to-fawn-to-brown
her neat crisp hair.
She was all clean, with that
iberian, genevese clean-ness
that makes it a lyrical cry.
Shining but calm she was,
her mind like her manners
calmly shining too.

What could she have been — 24?
in the mid-sixties when Castilian tyranny
began to thaw, in patches,
deceptive, cat-an'-mouse;
but at last, in some shops,
even in some shop-windows,
books in her native tongue:
la vella plata, the long-
banned speech

we talked in, she and I,
when once a week I came
to that so clean but bleakly clean
crucifyingly un-
lyrical office to put
into the tongue of an even fatter
conqueror than old Castile
a bunch of business-letters for her boss:
black sleeked-back short-
back-an'-sides tight corseted-looking
battleship-dull-dark business suit, civility —

oh such
        sleek bleak civility

(not in our native tongues) he needed me
like a hole in the head I needed him
even less he needed my English bad
I needed his filthy shekels

and so I trudged on sweltering foot
or strap-hanging in jam-packed creaking shuddering
falling-to-bits buses with people who had to
suffer that all life long
for a pittance — at least
he paid me well, and I could leave —
to that high, airy office with such a vantage over
the noisy, beautiful, grasping, lickerish, gallant,
irresistible city
                    hating
having to serve big business but worst of all
proud admanship Oh
how innocent even they
were then
                    compared to now
when their child-abuse and youth-abuse
conquer the small screen every brainwashed evening

but Enriqueta was nearly always there
to briefly crisply shake my hand to welcome
me in to the hateful office it almost seemed
like a real welcome she was so
neat and clean and civilized but never
indiscreet nor never
put a word wrong in the wrong
earshot then one day
she took our courage in her hands and showed me
the big book she was reading:

El Crist de nou crucificat
Christ recrucified her own book
in her own tongue I'll never forget

the pride in her eyes in her quiet voice
telling me Salas had done it straight
from Greek not second-hand. She lent it to me
a heavy book to swelter home with but
I juked into the not-quite-nearest pub
and over a cheap, rotgut glass
began to read, soon knowing her right:
for here was Catalan as crisp and rich as
Rovira i Virgili,
               Auziàs,
                       Sabaz —
though Franco was still
crucifying Christ for years to come.

I kept it far too long but gave it back when
I could not stand bleak admanship no longer
but all that year-or-so of trudging
to boost the adman I kept looking forward
to competent kindness. They'd have kept me
waiting a month for payment,
she knew my need and forced
cash on delivery. While I waited
for ten minutes or half-an-hour
in that bleak dazzling office I sometimes thought
of men who'd never see their country again
because they loved it as much as Enriqueta.
I never spoke to her of them,
there wasn't time — perhaps no need —
perhaps she knew
exiles at home,
neither in exile nor at home.

When competent kindness wasn't there, I'd leave
down-in-the-mouth, the nearest pub with tick
half-an-hour's weary walk away I never
summoned the courage to ask her out for a drink
just as well no doubt but Enriqueta

Enriqueta Bru
you were as crisp and lovely as
you were even finer
than your lovely name.

A Girl in Jerez de la Frontera, in the Autumn of 1952

Lank brownish hair,
and from under a pale-grey shift
only a faint
breast-sign;
her bare limbs thin, limp,
and the oldest face I ever saw,
the most hopeless,
scored by misery,
no gleam at all in her eyes.

Standing in the barber-shop doorway as I was leaving,
she asked me if I wanted her.
I asked how much.

'Un duro,' a five-peseta coin —
the rate was 160 to the pound.

I asked her age.
'Eleven.'

And looking down at her
I believed it.
Poverty, like love, works wonders.

Impeccably, Andalusianly, shaven,
I gave her some money —
can't remember exactly
but not much more than a duro —
and made for the nearest bar.

Duro is slang for a coin.
In the dictionary duro means hard.

Pilgrim

An old, blind, grey-haired, black pilgrim,
his left hand gripping a staff his own height,
almost as if planting it,
his garment grey-and-white,
                                        leaving bare
a strong left shoulder. He stands —
with his back to the dream's gaze —
framed in the frame of a door
but there's no door,
                              only that iron rectangle
the pilgrim is standing in, the dream
has no notion of where he has come through,
how long he's been standing there —
as if gazing out
over the vast whitegrey desert in front,
the endless desert —
and that was all there was to the dream:
no movement,
                        a still picture
that seemed to last for ever.

That was months ago, now looking back
the man who dreamt it can still see,
as clearly as in that night,
beggar perhaps and pilgrim —
no begging-bowl, no scallop-shell — an old black,
strong, blind man
standing free of iron,
alone, gripping a staff.

Judengasse

Over lunch at the long table in the lakeside castle
      someone names
         a Judengasse.
To which another says:
'It's an empty lane.'

Four of us by dusk we're in the city
      pub-crawling our way
         to the Jewish lane.
At midnight we've got to the mouth of it,
Lars and Folke and I, all in our early twenties,
and the novelist William Sansom,
an older man.

We're standing looking down the deserted, narrow,
longish, nearly-but-not-quite-straight
once Jewish lane.

No human light there now,
no sign of houses or workshops,
alive or empty.
Seven years after the war,
only the moon to glisten
the wet ground
of an empty lane.

Sansom is dark-haired, portly, a little flushed.
He's tightly encased in a dark suit, with a dark tie and
      a white shirt.
Impeccable. Handsome. Not undebonair.

Suddenly without a word
he up-ends himself, launches, flailing,
into a series of cartwheels along the wet lane to
      its empty end,

then barely pausing repeats the performance all the
    way back again
to land at our feet, exhausted.

We help him up, and back to the dead bishop's castle.

He spends the next day in bed.
I want to tell him I never admired him more.
But that were too banal an infringement
of friendliness so tightly encased.

A year or so later, Swiss Cottage,
he gave me a Jewish lunch.
Chicken livers with lemon I'd never eaten before.
They positively melted in the mouth.

The Most Beautiful Dog

for David Ferrer

A small dark bar on Vallirana, that long narrow street that climbs towards the foothills. You went down two or three steps from the blazing pavement into comparative coolness. Then, as like as not, you had to circumnavigate the massive dog that lay — all white but for a dab of dove-grey here and there — right in the middle of the floor, between low table and bar-counter. There was just about room to get past.

This magnificent creature sometimes rose to his full height, and stood there patiently while I stroked his thick, soft, immaculate white coat. Then he padded slowly away to the back shop. I always watched him, avidly, till he was out of sight. He was the most beautiful dog I've ever seen.

His name was Noi. The Catalan for boy. When I talked about him, and the small, old couple who ran the bar, to one of the regulars in the Bar-Bodega Vendrell, in the nearby Calle San Eusebio, he told me they'd never had any children. 'Noi is like their son,' he said. 'He *is* their son.'

It always did me good to sit and drink a glass or two in that small dark bar, watching the soft, white, massive beauty of that Pyrenean mastiff glowing softly, not blazing, while the small, drab-clad old pair moved like slow shadows behind the counter, from back shop to bar, occasionally quietly addressing their only child by his lovely name: 'Noi, noi . . . '

In Praise of Owls

*in memory of Norah Golden who gave me an owl-coaster
and of Uxío Novoneyra who gave me an owl-poem*

The face of the masked barn owl
is like a split pear
with a black cherry
in either half.

The snowy owl, on the other hand,
is entirely white
with huge eyes of pure gold:
no snow
was ever so white,
nor could any metal
shine so.

A First Time

When for the first time she let him walk her home
it was four in the morning and then she wouldn't
let him walk the whole way after all,
so they kissed again just round the corner
from where she lived then after a minute
she moved her lips away and the boy gazing
beyond her shoulder saw the dawn beginning.
He'd never seen the dawn before at such an hour —
and it was grey for Christ's sake:
the dawn wasn't supposed to be grey —
but then she moved away, though only a little,
and looking at him seriously she said:
Do you want to see me?
The boy was younger than his 18 calendar years,
so it took him a minute to understand her —
but he walked home exulting along the Appian Way
knowing the day after tomorrow
he would for the first time see
another human being entirely naked,
though he still couldn't get over finding out
the dawn could be grey.
But when at last he *saw* her,
this woman who'd claimed from the teasing start
her breasts were beyond praise beautiful,
the afternoon sun was filling the whole room
and he knew that her breasts were
beyond praise beautiful.

Benediction

The boy was nearly always bored at Mass
except sometimes at the end
of twelve Mass on a Sunday
when monstrance-blazing, incense-billowing
Benediction raised its golden head
erupting into the church encrusted with
decades of dull stale greasy
shuffling muttering sound,
rescuing that young child
up from his numb trance of boredom onto
a wide-eyed sun-star lunette-glinting
botafumeiro smoky incensual trance of Alive!

You couldn't count on it, mind,
three Sundays often went by bereft of such wild blessing,
but when it did shine forth, for that small boy,
then Benediction
                           was Resurrection
raising him up from the tomb
the long flat Mass had buried him in.

Nelly Doody

Nelly Doody in Templeglantine
tended the holy wells.

From well to well she traipsed
lifelong.

From time to time she borrowed a ladder
from a farmyard —
and didn't always leave it back in time.

But well by well
every ladder-after-ladder on her back
was the cross He bore on His.
With water-meadow and rag-tree
she kept faith.

And Christ kept faith with her:
she'd always *said* she wanted to die
at three o'clock on Good Friday,
and *He* made sure she did.

Though now and again she borrowed a ladder
from a farmyard —
sometimes when the farmer wasn't looking —
but most of the farmers didn't mind too much:
they knew she was traipsing for them.
Maybe one or two cursed her, but

When Christ hauled her up beside him
all the ladders in Templeglantine
got the day off from the farmers
and wept into the wells.

The Miracle of Bread and Fiddles

We were so hungry
we turned bark into bread.

But still we were hungry,
so we turned clogs into fiddles.

Kent in Sussex

for Ivor Gurney and his patria chica

'The train was made from Kentish — '
I barely heard the rest but like
an old warhorse pricked up
my ears at that one ringing
Kentish!

(radio's loving recall
of regal wedding-gown —
'silkworms and woven in London')

Now not a fig care I
for sceptred empress or
for Agincourt, what that gave me
was loving recollection of —
almost as long ago
as that gone wedding-day —

a spry, sonsy, middle-aged, kindly
lodging-house-keeper in Seaford, Sussex,
that long, sunny weekend in summer
breakfast-bringing and when I asked her
'Where are you from?' she stepped away,
threw her head back, her eyes flashed —

'I'm a Kentish girl myself.'

That proud cry
still ringing through my brain as young
I stepped it out along the high green sward
above white cliffs, the undulating
Seven Sisters, headland yielding
to green-white headland, the sun's light
not Middle-Sea not blinding
no but buoyant and soothing —

Oh if only the stranger on the train,
as it trundled through the all-but-Spanish-coloured
Sussex Downs,
when I,
fresh from interminable journeys on Spanish trains
where everybody asked everybody else about their patria
chica,
asked him where he was from,
had instead of getting embarrassed
cried out proud:
'I'm a Kentish girl myself!'

Eel

Teaching English brought in precious little in June, July and August. So for several summers running Ernie abandoned the city and worked as a tourist-guide on the Costa Brava.

One day in Calella he escaped from his charges, and went for a stroll — away from the esplanade, the crowds, the snapshots. That was in the mid-sixties, and in those days many Catalan resorts, inundated for months by foreign visitors, nonetheless contrived to keep, half-hidden away, a real village, a native core. That was partly what Ernie was looking for, and above all he wanted a small, reasonably quiet bar, where instead of English or German another tongue might be heard: Castilian maybe? or even, mirabile dictu, Catalan.

Before finding any such bar, what he found, as he turned a corner from one narrow sidestreet into another, was a sidewalk stall displaying the fruits of the sea, and standing beside it a sonsy girl of 15 or 16, who was clutching an eel tight just under the head and kissing it repeatedly and telling it tenderly: 'Oi qu'ets formós! Oi qu'ets formós!' (How beautiful you are! How beautiful you are! . . .)

'I envied that eel,' said Ernie when he'd told me, his blond beard curling with amusement.

Vincent de Paul, Dublin 1946

Crouching in a corner
completely naked
a small, old man
completely hairless
cowering, quivering
in a grey room
as naked as him
his hands covering
between his legs

his moving living
body so white
in the dull grey
unmoving space
his eyes so frightened
pleading up at us
we visited in pairs
to save our souls

We must have reported it
at the next meeting
in Ozanam House
but all I remember
is an old naked man
alone for ever
on a hard floor
terrified

11/8/2001

Manifesto

Universal courtesy —
now that would be
revolutionary

A Findrum Blackbird

Were there nightingales here before the Adze-head croziered?
and maybe she left us
alongwith the serpent?
How should a snake and a nightingale con*sort*?
She hardly wrenned it on his eagle-back,
unless he was Mexican — or did she guide him
back to the garden of eden?

But never mind, we have the blackbird still —
de Ierse nachtegaal, as Johann Jacob van Eyck
might well have called him,
peddling all over flanders unearthly flute-music —
what nightingale could ever sing
so well as that blind wanderer?

Perched acrest a lilac-bush
just inside the front gate
black-and-yellow music
turns a garden into a glade-scriptorium,
brings back those pagan monks,
and fills my deaf harmonious kitchen-window
with yellow-and-black music.

For Alan

Walking home tonight
thinking about you, a poem about you
began in my head and by the time
I was halfway home it was finished. I said it
all 8 or 11 lines again
and gave it, for the time being, an imprimatur.
You've no idea, my lost dear,
how much that cheered me up.
But by the time I got home,
that poem had vanished.
Poems come and go — like you.
Not like you.
The old mind is gone.
But every time I turn that corner,
your arm is there, your mind is mine,
your caution, as great as mine,
your courage so much much greater;
and that's not the same poem at all —

Ten Months Later

In a bereft room
forgetting the dead for a while
Music arrives on the radio
music he loved
His never-again enjoyment
I used to love it too
How can I enjoy it now?
Cruelty garottes
heart-lifting sound

Two Young Men

Two young men in Belfast fell in love,
hands reaching out in real peace
across the dangerous peace-line.
They gave each other pleasure —
maybe even happiness, who knows? —
and one day the protestant lad
gave his catholic lover
a plant for his window-sill,
a warm geranium.

Then the catholic street was torched,
and the catholic boy killed.
His lover ran both gauntlets
across the god-fearing city
and rescued back, against the odds,
that plant of trust,
his flower of love.

That flower was all his own now,
his loss replete.

2000

Fear

for Jaime Sabines

Fear kills.
The dead kill.

Some courage
beats fear.

Loving the dead
can kill.

Not to love them
is the worst death.

Some courage
beats fear.

Can fear
beat love?

One of the Finest Things

After a few days I began to find Toledo a bit claustrophobic. So I went for a walk outside the city walls.

But had to cut it short. The sky was cloudless, and that was what I'd always wanted; but another old craving, the heat, was for once too intense.

So there I was, walking back towards Toledo along a broad, high, dusty road confined, on one side by a low parapet overlooking a fearsome gorge, and on the other by a towering wall, when all of a sudden just in front of me an emerald-green lizard shot out from the parapet at the speed of light, and vanished into the wall opposite.

I can't have glimpsed it for more than a couple of seconds but it filled my astonished, enraptured eyes, and still does; it glowed and sparkled, pure clean-looking emerald-green, as if freshly washed for all the desolating dryness surrounding us on all sides; its rich-green glory put to shame those greys and fawns and bits of grass sucked dry of colour.

I can still see that flash of emerald-green as vivid as it was that afternoon nearly fifty years ago, I still remember it as one of the finest things.

River

for Sujata Bhatt

She plucked a flower and leaving the village
walked as far as the river.
She stood for a minute, watching the water move,
then bending down she placed — not cast —
the flower on the water.
Standing there for a short while, relaxing,
she watched the river carry the flower away,
till it was out of sight beyond the trees.
Then she walked back home.

Notes and Acknowledgements

The dedication in *Tongue without Hands* read 'for my Mother'; in *Watching the Morning Grow* 'to Maurice O'Dwyer (1932-1972)'; in *Climbing the Light* 'to Justin O'Mahony (1943-1979)'; and in *Barnsley Main Seam* 'for Alan Biddle (Kircubbin 1952 - Dublin 1994)'.

The epigraph in *Expansions* read ' . . . les obscenes expansions de la vanitat' — Salvador Espriu (the obscene expansions of vanity).

'Cat Rua' appeared in the *Cork Examiner*. Some of 'New Poems' appeared in *Chapman, Cyphers* and *Poetry Ireland Review*. 'In Praise of Owls' was published separately by The Gallery Press.

page 20   *horse-magog*: a Scots word meaning a rollicking, boisterous, boastful type of a man.

page 34   *Bragitóir*: In medieval Ireland, a kind of buffoon who entertained his audience by farting (Kuno Meyer says). In the *Leabhar Buidhe*, in an older form, this definition appears: Brigedóirí. i. do niad an bruigedóracht as a tónaibh.

          Bousingot: Nom donné en France, après la revolution de 1830, à des jeunes gens (Nerval, Gautier, etc) qui affichaient des opinions très démocratiques (peut-être à cause du chapeau et du costume excentriques qu'ils avaient adoptés). — Hatzfeld and Darmesteter. It previously meant a sailor's hat, and that, according to Ch. Nisard, came from 'bousin' (originally English 'bowsing') — sailor's argot for a cabaret or dive.

page 44   *An Nollaig sa tSamhradh*: Christmas in Summer. From a love-song by Seán Ó Neachtain (1655-1728), Roscommon-born poet and novelist.

page 60   The Castilian in line 3 means: a gentle, or tame, blind man. Mansísimo, in line 4, is the superlative of manso. ('Toro manso' means a fighting bull that refuses to fight.)

page 64   In the first line of verse 2, cul-d'jatte (which might be Englished as 'jarse') is, or was, a French term for someone with no legs who was strapped into a jar or bowl, or onto a board with wheels, propelling it along with the hands. Billy-in-the-Bowl, or the blind cripple in Buñuel's Mexican film, 'Los Olvidados'.

page 71 In line 2, Cour des Myrtes is French for the Court-yard, or Patio, of Myrtles, in the Alhambra. My guidebook was the Guide Bleu. Riviera dei Fiori: the Riviera of Flowers. Riviera delle Palme: the Riviera of Palmtrees. Via dei Fiori Oscuri: the Street of Dark Flowers. Via dei Fiori Chiari: the Street of Bright Flowers.

page 77 The epigraph, in Castilian, means: I've seen good people everywhere.

page 80 'Speaking to Some' records only part of the un-comprehending animosity that anyone with a beard was bound to be on the receiving end of in the 1950s anywhere in Western Europe. In my own experience, The Hague, Barcelona, and Palma de Mallorca were the worst.

Everything described in this poem happened to me in the latter pair of otherwise delightful cities, though it was only in The Hague that the taunting became so bad and so constant that I lay for three days in bed, miserably gazing at the ceiling, not daring to go out. In the early 60s a little civiliza-tion began to reappear, in this regard at least.

pp 87/88 The Catalan epigraph, from the poem 'Infants' (Children) means: their civil war against the giants. On page 88, 'Das ist nicht möglich' is perhaps best translated as: That cannot be.

page 92 The Gaelic means, in verse 1: The Gaelic is less than the water in that glass; in verse 3: I speak with strangers. I believe it's right to be speaking with strangers. (Strangers, here, has the sense of outlanders, foreigners, runners-in.) In verse 4: Ah, son: don't be breaking a boat. This last was said to my friend Liam Brady in Carraroe.

page 95 The Gaelic sentence the painter spoke, in my hearing, means: You think I am out of my mind. That the 'you' is plural is plain in Gaelic, though not in what Auden calls 'the Oxonian dialect'. The Dublin 'yous' or the Munster 'ye' would be clearer.

page 98   For the 'tibi' in the dedication, see Catullus, who isn't otherwise relevant. I use it to address Cornelius Kavanagh, in and about whose parents' home these lines were written when he was two.

page 108 merkin: US term for a pubic wig; nobilities: in parts of Spain male genitals are called 'noblezas'; a cristazos limpios: Franco's bully-boys used this term themselves; it means with clean Christ-blows, or Christings.

pp 111/112 The Gaelic line in verse 4 means: but they didn't taste Mary and they didn't see Christ; and in verse 6: may they never taste drink and never see Christ. This Gaelic is for rhyme and macaronic.

page 113 'a tremble of light in the leaves' is a translation of a Castilian phrase from an essay by Unamuno. Prou: Catalan for enough, basta! Recostracullóns: a bilingual oath I first came across in the Valencian Blasco Ibáñez's novel 'La Barraca'. Costra is Castilian for crust, and cullóns (with strong emphasis on the second syllable) is a frequent exclamation in Barcelona; the literal meaning is 'balls'. The composite word would have much the same effect as the French 'Merde, remerde, et outremerde!'

page 115 This was written the day after she was arrested.

page 124 Martí (Havana, 1853-Dos Ríos, 1895), who died for the freedom of Cuba, wrote a book of poems called 'Versos Sencillos', from which came the words of the song 'Guantanamera', and from the longest poem in which I've taken these verses.

page 125 Sant Jordi (Saint George) is the patron saint of Catalonia, and on his feast-day the custom is for friends and lovers to give each other a rose and a book.

pp 126/127 In verse 2, the lines 'oh truly dead, oh my darling Queralt, / far from your high native rock' refer to Josep Queralt i Clapes from Badalona, a Catalan patriot and Spanish republican who lived in the old Catalan town of Perpinyà (French: Perpignan) from the end of the Civil War till his death in 1966. The name Queralt, he explained to me, is made up of 'quer', a now obsolete word meaning 'rock', and 'alt', meaning 'high'. For three of the last four years I lived in Barcelona, he was a rock for me, a rock of shelter and hope. A second father. Four times a year, his home was mine. In verse 2, line 13, 'the pigeon-in-cabbage' was cooked by his Pyrenean wife, Antonyeta Pedra — one of the two best cooks I ever knew.

The Gaelic lines in verse 3, from a poem by Seán Ó Neachtain (see note *page* 44), mean: The eagle's on top of the pine-tree and the corncrake's in the nettles. In verse 4, trandafír is one of the Rumanian names for a rose.

page 128   Kuruntokai is a collection of Tamil love-poems.

page 129   The first country is Transylvania; I read a book about it twenty years ago and, to my shame, I've forgotten both title and author. The second country is Ireland, my authority Dinneen. The third country is Guatemala, which I read about in Luís Cardoza y Aragón's 'Guatemala: en las líneas de su mano' (Fondo de Cultura Económica, Mexico).

page 138   Boxing the fox: Dublin slang for robbing an orchard.

page 140   Pòl Crùbach MacLeoid: Scots Gaelic poet (fl 1650).

page 146   The Spanish epigraph, from the Mexican poet Octavio Paz, means: In you I eat sun.

page 147   Posada: 19th-century Mexican cartoonist, especially famous for his festive skeletons (dancing, carousing, making love in flowering hats).

page 150   Bràfim: a village in Catalonia, where the common name is not red wine but vi negre (black wine). Queluz: a town in Portugal, where there's a wine called vinho verde (green wine). Auzias March: Catalan poet (1397-1457), born in Gandia, Valencia. Martim Codax: Galaico-Portuguese poet of the fourteenth-century. Sueca: village in Valencia. Anselm Turmeda: Majorcan Franciscan who went to Tunis and became a Muslim. Up to the nineteenth century he was still venerated there as a saint of Islam. The monolith: Castile, of which Azorín (himself a Valencian, writing in Castilian) once said: Castile is thirsty for the sea.

from Spain. And: Hardiman quotes (in his book *Irish Minstrelsy*), a note by Nash to his edition of 'Hudibras': 'At Cashel in the County of Tipperary, stormed by Lord Inchiquin in the civil wars, there were near 700 put to the sword . . . Among the slain of the Irish were found, when stripped, divers that had tails near a quarter of a yard long. Forty soldiers, who were eye-witnesses, testified the same upon their oaths.'

page 171 The black sticks of the devil: from one of the *dis*-approving Gaelic names for the pipes: maidí dubha an diabhail. Barcelona: the Catalan poet Salvador Espriu has a line, 'tornar a les coses el seu nom' (to give things back their name), and walking one day in Barcelona I realized it might mean, quite simply, to put the street-names in Catalan, not in Castilian, the language of the conqueror. Belfast: the name is an anglicization of the original Gaelic, Béal Feirste.

page 174 'In July, two hundred people of Ross, thirty-three families and twenty-five single men, boarded the *Hector* at Ullapool on Loch Broom. The ship was so rotten that the emigrants were able to pick away its timbers with their fingernails . . . The people left in good spirits, and when their piper was ordered ashore because he had no money to pay for his passage "they pleaded to have him allowed to accompany them, and offered to share their rations with him in exchange for his music . . . " In Nova Scotia they went ashore behind their piper, wearing the tartan that was still under proscription in Scotland.' (John Prebble: *The Highland Clearances*, Penguin, 1969)

page 178 Macdara, a Christian name (and the name of a saint who has an island called after him), means: the son of the oak-tree. The Gaelic sentence means: 'Son, don't be breaking a cat: she'll be broken soon enough.' This may seem harsh — not much better, indeed, than calling the pony Leprechaun — but in fact it was an irresistible echo of the remark 'Ah son, don't be breaking a boat', made (in Irish) to my friend Liam Brady in

Connemara, and quoted in an earlier poem of mine (see 'Gaeltacht', *page 92*).

page 179 The island of Mallorca had been under Catalan rule since 1229. On the 2nd of August, 1391, 'diada de la Mare de Déu dels Àngels' (the Feast of Our Lady of the Angels), over six thousand country-people poured into Palma in revolt against regal — and also episcopal — injustice. The authorities managed to divert their anger onto the Jewish quarter. Three hundred Jews were killed. One result was that the Jews were forbidden to practise their religion, own property, or possess arms. By the end of 1391, there had, naturally enough, been many 'conversions'. The story and the names I found in Baltasar Porcel's book on the Jews of his native Mallorca, 'Los chuetas mallorquines' (Barral, Barcelona, 1971).

page 181 The phrase 'in your enlightened times' refers to the long tyranny of Franco, under which Catalan was forbidden, and only the Castilian forms of first names were officially accepted. Gaietà is Catalan, Cayetano Castilian. Gaietà Ripoll was a Catalan schoolmaster, born about 1778. In 1824 he was teaching in Ruçafa, imparting evangelical ideas. A pious woman denounced him to the Inquisition for not bringing his pupils to Mass or making them kneel at the passing of the Host. Locked up and interrogated for two years, he refused to recant. He shared both his clothes and his food with his fellow-prisoners. On the 29th June, 1826, in Valencia, he was condemned to be hanged (over the cardboard flames), as 'a dogmatizing heretic and perverter of youth'. The sentence was carried out twenty-four hours later. His last words, 'Crec en Déu', mean, in Catalan, 'I believe in God'. By the time the Editorial Selecta, of Barcelona, published Jordi Ventura's book, 'Els heretges catalans' (The Catalan Heretics) in 1963, there was a certain thaw in the ban on Catalan; but it still took courage to bring out a book on such a theme.

pp 182/183 'The Kid on the Mountain' is the name of a slip-jig. 'A tremble of light in the leaves': see note *page* 113.

page 185   Amhrán na mBréag: The Song of Lies. Also known as An t-Amhrán Bréagach: The Lying Song. Songs of this kind used to be quite common in Irish. They were often used as lullabies. Bréagadh, as a verb, means to cajole, coax, or soothe. Whatever about their uses, though, it's clear that these songs allowed the people who made them up to give free rein to their imagination. I just lifted lines I liked from three or four examples in *Clár Amhrán Bhaile na hInse* by Ríonach Ní Fhlathartaigh (An Clóchomhar, 1976). Mícheál Mharcais is the only author named, and his version was collected by Éamonn Ó Conghaile from Beartla Ó Conghaile, of Cárna in Connemara, in 1952.

page 191   Emma Goldman (1869-1940) went from Russia to the United States of America when she was seventeen. By the turn of the century she was a famous anarchist leader. At the end of the 1914-1918 war, during which she had been a pacifist, she was deported back to Russia. Her massive and magnificent autobiography, *Living My Life*, was first published by Knopf in 1931, and re-issued by Dover in 1970. In Chapter 52 she vividly describes her meeting in Moscow in 1920 with Maria Spiridonovna, who was by that time even more disillusioned with Lenin than Emma herself was becoming. It's from this account that I got the main matter of this poem, including the cherries and Maria's parting gesture. According to Goldman, Spiridonovna was a member of the Socialist Revolutionary Party, and in 1905, at the age of eighteen, had carried out her party's instructions to kill General Lukhanovsky, governor of Tambov Province, 'the notorious executioner of the peasants'. She was sentenced to death, but international protest got this commuted to Siberian exile for life. Released in 1917, she — like most of her party — soon broke with the Bolsheviks, 'considering peace with the Kaiser a fatal betrayal of the Revolution'. She was arrested, imprisoned, escaped, re-arrested, re-imprisoned, released because she was ill. When Emma Goldman met her she was, despite her release, on the run. Like the country-people who wrote to her, she 'had taken the meaning and purpose of the soviets literally', and they wouldn't wear the Bolshevik middlemen: the commissars.

Antonio Machado once wrote to Unamuno that he never finished a poem without at once wanting to write another one to contradict it. I feel a bit like that about this poem, though 'contradict' might be putting it too strongly.

page 193   The Gaelic in lines 8 and 9 means: 'you simpleton! you finished fool!' ('finished' here standing for utter, out-an'-out). Under 'pleidhce', Ó Dónaill simply gives 'simpleton, fool'; but the entry for the same word in Dinneen (whose great work Ó Dónaill himself has rightly described as a thesaurus) begins like this: 'a stump or stake, a flake, a roll, a bundle of rolls of carded wool (about as many as would be put together in a dildurn); a fool . . . '

pp 197/198   The title is that of an old Chinese tune. The other titles quoted in the poem are mainly those of Irish tunes and English pubs — though there's also one herb and one painting: Bruegel's *The Magpie on the Gallows* (1568), now in the Hessisches Landesmuseum in Darmstadt. 'According to Van Mander, Bruegel means here that those who speak evil should be condemned to the gallows . . . in an idyllic landscape stands the gallows with the magpie on it, while to the left peasants are dancing. Van Bastelaer sees in the theme a reference to the situation of the Netherlands, where all that seemed serene was potentially dangerous. Faggin interprets the subject as an allegory of the despotism of Philip II, which could never succeed in depriving the Flemish people of the sun or of the joy of living; and he sees the work as a triumph of light and air.' (Arturo Bovi: *Bruegel*. Thames and Hudson, London, 1971)

Darach Ó Catháin was one of the greatest of Gaelic singers. I was with him when the barman said that.

When Stalin was on the run before the Revolution, he went by the name Koba.

pp 201/202 The phrase 'mo bhrón géar' means: my sharp sorrow (bh = v). In 'drúchtín' the *ch* is guttural, as in loch. Here's part of what Dinneen has to say about it: 'a light dew; a dewdrop; a species of small whitish snail, a slug . . . On May morning girls discovered the colour of the hair of their future husbands from the shade of colouring of the first drúichtín they found . . . Mar d'fheartaibh an drúchtín tsúrthaoi an crannchur sin, / Ní h-aithreach atú tríd shiubhal Laoi Bealltaine', since by the virtues of the white slug you seek that destiny, I do not regret your May morning's walk (H.) . . . ' H. is Pádraigín Haicéad, who (unlike Dinneen but like Ó Dónaill now) spells drúchtín without the first *i*.

Iron Crow: Crossmaglen term for helicopter.

Five Grey Sisters: stained-glass windows in Yorkminster.

Barnsley Main Seam: a small model, in a glass case, of men working away at the coal-face, it's tucked unobtrusively into a wall amid the Gothic splendours; and the caption beneath it reads: 'The tribute of the miners of Yorkshire to the Minster.'

Deopdale: 'Deep', in the present spelling, is just a corruption of an old word meaning dale.

The Gaelic in the last two lines means: 'for she took the summer with her for ever'. 'Thugamar féin an samhradh linn' is an old Irish May-day song, usually sung by young girls.

page 220 She fell asleep in the sun: I owe this expression to the poet and scholar Dáithí Ó hÓgáin, who found it for me in the archives of Roinn Bhéaloideas Éireann (the Department of Irish Folklore), University College, Dublin. For that and for other things in the same context I'm grateful to him, as I am to Áine McEvoy (the woman from Kerry) who gave me that incomparable phrase 'leanbh ón ngréin', and to my friend from Tiernahilla (County Limerick), the poet Pádraig de Vál, for the line 'garsúinín beag mishtake'.

page 222 Een fenster is alles = a window is all. The Flemish poet Paul van Ostaijen was born in 1896 and died in 1928.

page 237 In the last verse, line 2, 'Where the Air is Clear' means Mexico City. It's the title of the English translation of the novel by Carlos Fuentes which first made him famous, namely 'La región más transparente del aire' – literally, 'the most transparent region of the air'. In other words, Mexico City. I can't think of any translation more brilliantly found, so different, so much more crisp and lyrical, yet entirely faithful.

page 239 This poem is for Paddy Joe Hill, because on that memorable day in 1991, when the Birmingham Six finally came out of court vindicated, one of the first things he said to the world was: 'It's English justice, not British — we can't blame the Scots or the Welsh.'

page 252 Pulcherrima Paradigmata = resplendent paradigms. A phrase remembered from Erigena. I couldn't resist it.

page 256 La vella plata = the old silver. The Catalan poet Salvador Espriu used it to mean the Catalan language.

page 265 The artist Norah Golden was born in Oldham, lived in Ballydehob for many years, and died in Romsey in 1997.

page 267 In line 12, the Galician word 'botafumeiro' refers to the giant thurible in the great pilgrim cathedral of Santiago de Compostela.

page 275 An Tál-cheann (the Adze-head) was an early Gaelic nickname for St Patrick, inspired by the shape of his mitre. De Ierse nachtegaal (the Irish nightingale) is adapted from De Engelse nachtegaal (the English nightingale), one of the loveliest airs of that great Flemish composer, Jacob van Eyck.